PENGUIN BUSINESS

THE DOLPHIN AND THE SHARK

Namita Thapar is an MBA from the Fuqua School of Business and a chartered accountant from the Institute of Chartered Accountants of India. She joined Emcure as CFO, after her six-year stint at Guidant Corporation, USA. Subsequently, her responsibilities grew to manage Emcure's largest business unit: the India business. Namita is passionate about improving women's health in India and promoting youth entrepreneurship. During the COVID pandemic, she launched a unique YouTube talk show on women's health called *Uncondition Yourself with Namita*, which aims to provide authentic information and break taboos associated with women's health. She leads Thapar Entrepreneurs Academy Ltd, an education company that teaches entrepreneurship. She is the founding partner of Thapar Vision Fund, which invests in start-ups. Namita is a recipient of various prestigious corporate awards, such as the 40 Under Forty award by *Economic Times* and Top 50 Most Powerful Women in Business by *Business Today*. She has been a speaker at various prestigious forums, such as the Harvard Business School, the Indian Institute of Management Ahmedabad, ET Women's Forum and FICCI, etc. She lives in Pune with her husband, Vik, and two boys, Vir and Jai. This is her first book.

THE
DOLPHIN
AND THE
SHARK

STORIES ON
ENTREPRENEURSHIP

NAMITA
THAPAR

BUSINESS

An imprint of Penguin Random House

PENGUIN BUSINESS

USA | Canada | UK | Ireland | Australia
New Zealand | India | South Africa | China

Penguin Business is part of the Penguin Random House group of companies
whose addresses can be found at global.penguinrandomhouse.com

Published by Penguin Random House India Pvt. Ltd
4th Floor, Capital Tower 1, MG Road,
Gurugram 122 002, Haryana, India

First published in Penguin Business by Penguin Random House India 2022

ISBN 9780143458975

Typeset in Adobe Caslon Pro by MAP Systems, Bengaluru, India

www.penguin.co.in

This book is dedicated to my family and my mentors who taught me to believe in myself!

Stories inspire, stories lift.

I have been lucky to have been part of several stories, either in person or through books. These have shaped me and put that fire in my belly.

These are not entrepreneurship lessons but rather stories that I hope will inspire you to push your limits!

Contents

Preface

When I signed up for *Shark Tank India*, I had no idea it would take the country by storm and result in a movement that celebrates the spirit of entrepreneurship! Two months of hectic shooting and learning without any playbook was followed by a couple of months of watching the show and learning from that as well. Once everything was in place sometime around mid-February 2022, all those amazing stories and experiences were buzzing in my head. Hours of sitting by my son for moral support while he studied for his ICSE boards gave me the perfect opportunity to turn into a writer. What you have in your hands today is a result of that.

The goal of writing this book is to share stories; stories that will, hopefully, inspire and lift.

The title is very close to my heart. I strongly believe that all of us have a shark in us representing aggression, ruthlessness and ferocity. At the same time, we also have a dolphin within representing kindness, empathy and vulnerability. We have to learn to balance both if we want to maximize our productivity and potential.

I always believed in the adage, 'Work towards leaving the place a little better than when you found it . . .' To me, entrepreneurship enables this. I have seen my father, a first-generation entrepreneur, endure struggles and setbacks, only to go on and build an INR 6900-crore global pharma behemoth with over 10,000 employees and presence in over seventy countries. I know how important it is to support entrepreneurs as I have witnessed first-hand how the support my father received in his early days was largely instrumental in his success. Along with my role at Emcure, where I am busy building large brands as the India business head, I always had an itch to do that extra bit to support entrepreneurs. Entrepreneurship has the power to democratize wealth creation in our country which will undoubtedly bring in the next wave of economic development and prosperity. Much needed now more than ever, after the COVID pandemic setback. Needless to say, when the *Shark Tank India* opportunity came my way—through sheer chance from a distant network—I grabbed it with both hands and plunged in with all my head and heart. Here was an opportunity to make a difference, to create an impact and highlight India's success stories on an international canvas. I was both excited and nervous.

Every story amidst these pages has been written by me, in my own words and straight from the heart. I requested my publishers to keep the editing to a bare minimum so that we could retain the authenticity and rawness that I wanted.

In the initial chapters, I have shared stories from *Shark Tank India* Season 1; journeys of a few Indian entrepreneurs, and glimpses from my professional life at Emcure peppered with personal anecdotes. The chapters on investment framework, perfecting your pitch and what next after you get a deal will hopefully help start-up founders early in their company's journey, especially with respect to fundraising. Chapters on teams, brands and dissent are relevant not just for start-ups but for any enterprise looking to scale. Chapters on mentors, networks, leadership mantras, the 3Cs, the vulnerable leader and the lifelong learner are about honing your work and leadership style. Entrepreneurship is a lonely and stressful journey and these chapters may help one maintain a broader outlook and balance while continuing to grow personally and professionally. Chapters on family business and breaking barriers are more specific and situational. They, however, are very relevant—common but yet to be addressed in-depth. Hopefully, this book has something for entrepreneurs as well as aspiring entrepreneurs.

I hope you enjoy these pages and get inspired to scale newer heights in your journeys.

After all, life is an experience and not an enquiry!

Chapter 1

Why This Book: My Story

So ... why this book? As I stated earlier, I had all these stories inside of me that I felt the need to express. Learnings from inspiring people I have met, my mentors and their lessons, my own life experiences and how I have evolved over the years. This book is primarily meant for entrepreneurs but also for students and anyone else interested in learning more about entrepreneurship. The lessons included in the book are not just for founders but also for those who want to scale existing businesses in this increasingly complex world.

In this chapter, I would like to bring my story to life and talk about how *Shark Tank India* seemed to be a calling that all of my life's small and big experiences were subconsciously preparing me for.

Rocky Start

I was born in a traditional Gujarati joint family in the then sleepy town of Pune, a hub for students and retirees. We had a simple childhood without the distractions of television and social media. There are three distinct experiences or memory sets from my childhood that, I believe, have shaped me. Firstly, I was the eldest among nine grandkids. Securing the first rank in class was not only important but expected. I remember the period of summer vacations when all nine of us would be spending time together; awaiting the arrival of report cards. Apart from me, everyone else always stood first in their respective classes. I was never congratulated for coming in second or securing whatever rank I had. Instead, the entire discussion would be around where the gap was and what could be done to bridge it. A subject-by-subject analysis would ensue and an action plan would be created. It was among the reasons for my low self-esteem as a teen.

Then, of course, being overweight and name-calling by others including being teased as a *'mishi wali porgi'* (Marathi) which meant 'the girl with the moustache' didn't help. These incidents, have, however, built my character and made me an empath.

I have often spoken about my second set of experiences or memories. My mother got married into a joint family at the age of twenty. All through her twenties and thirties, she assumed the responsibility of working tirelessly and making sacrifices to support a struggling entrepreneurial husband. I still remember those days when there would be buckets all over our home, collecting rainwater from our dripping roof. Yet, my mom would insist that my father's business contacts come home for lunch and not dinner to avoid the onslaught of mosquitoes in the evenings. She lived all her unfulfilled dreams through bedtime stories narrated to her daughter. She meticulously cut pictures from magazines and newspapers and put them all over my room—pictures of career women in crisp business suits, with briefcases, immaculate hair and make-up and high heels, making presentations, on calls, looking in charge and powerful.

Those images are clearly imprinted on my mind even today. This instilled drive in me.

The final memory is that of my father experiencing losses year after year; being humiliated by many and asking my mother to tell creditors that he wasn't at home when they called. All through this, he never lost his cool or his smile, a lesson in resilience and positivity. I completed my CA at the age of 21 as tags mattered in my family. It helped that I loved math and accounting. My first paycheck came from my articleship at a Pune firm called Kirtane Pandit Chartered Accountants. It felt good to have my own money. However, for my young readers out there, I have another important story to tell in this context. Missing my 10th and 12th class board ranks pushed me into an extensive period of anxiety that eased only after I completed my CA. Looking back, I now see how I spent a majority of my teenage years defining my self-worth on the basis of a marksheet. How irrelevant that marksheet is today! Yet, I spent years being riddled with anxiety and crying rather than having fun, pursuing hobbies and building great childhood memories. After finishing up CA, I wanted to go abroad to do my MBA. I was the first girl from my family to do so before getting married.

Many well-intentioned relatives advised my parents against it but this is where their progressive outlook and ambition for their daughter overrode everything else. It is something that I will always have the deepest gratitude for. They overruled all naysayers and sent me to Duke University for my MBA when I was twenty-two. I was the youngest in my class; from a super protected environment back home and here I was, being thrown into this new world. I wouldn't say I thrived, but I definitely survived, given how lost and lonely I felt in those days.

Early Working Days

Getting a job fresh out of business school at a marquee health-care company in the Bay Area was among the best memories of my life. Using the sign-on bonus to buy my first gift for my parents was definitely a high point! These small, simple milestones bring a smile to my face even today. Working for six years in the US post my MBA is what truly defined my work ethic. In my chapter on family business, I have brought out how important it is for second generation family members to work outside their businesses. I learned a lot but yearned to move back to India.

Those who have lived away from their country will relate to the deep sense of longing that one experiences to go back to one's own roots—I felt that strongly in those days. I am not one to cry easily but I remember bawling as I watched the Shah Rukh Khan-starrer *Swades*. I married Vik in 2002. He is a US citizen who had no plans of ever moving to India but he saw my pain, my desire to move, and decided to give it a shot for a couple of years. He finally said 'yes' in late 2006. Vik left his comfort zone and took a chance and I will forever be grateful for that bold move.

What also helped is how brilliantly the Indian economy was shaping up in that decade and that Emcure was at the cusp of explosive growth with its very first institutional investment from a marquee private equity firm. Here was a unique opportunity to be part of the India growth story as well as contribute meaningfully to the upcoming transformation at Emcure. Needless to say, I was thrilled that we were moving to India. I have repeatedly said that when you want something with all your heart, the universe conspires to make it happen. I truly believe that moving to India after eight years of living in the US was one such moment.

I had worked for six years in the Silicon Valley, at a marquee company called Guidant Corporation that manufactured stents. I had worked in various senior roles in finance as well as marketing. I assumed that after two degrees and six years of work experience in the US, I would be welcomed with a certain degree of respect at Emcure. How wrong I was. The old-timers did not take me seriously and it took persistent efforts and outcomes to prove my credibility. I joined Emcure as the CFO. Over the next seven years, I proved my mettle in finance and delivered systems and processes along with improved profitability. However, when an opportunity to lead the India business opened up, my work as the CFO counted for nothing as I was labelled a 'finance' person with no sales experience. I had to go through hoops and was eventually given the job after a one-year probation. I worked harder than I ever had and got the sales numbers, and this role, on a permanent basis! Today, it fills me with pride that I run our high potential and profitable India business with 3000 medical representatives spanning seventeen therapeutic areas and have not only built big brands but truly made Emcure a purpose-driven organization in the healthcare space.

My journey at Emcure has been an exciting rollercoaster ride. I joined when we were an INR 500-crore company with almost all our sales from the India market. Today, as I write this, we are an INR 6900-crore company with 55 per cent of our sales from global markets. The good times have been great but it's the tough times which have been heart wrenching and taught me more. I wanted to use this book to tell a few of those stories. About how our manufacturing facility was banned from exporting to the US markets, what went wrong, and what we learned from that. About how we learned some hard lessons through our global acquisitions. About how laying off 300 representatives was one of the toughest things I have done as a leader, especially in terms of dealing with social media backlash and legal cases against me.

My Calling

Over time, I have defined three purposes in my life – moving the needle on healthcare, entrepreneurship and supporting women. In healthcare, I am making strides with Emcure. On the women empowerment front, I helped Niti Aayog with its Women Entrepreneurship Platform; started a learning and networking platform called 'Prerna' for women at Emcure; anchored a show on women's health called *Uncondition Yourself with Namita Thapar* and pushed our medical and marketing teams to scale our research and free diagnosis camps around women's health. However, I didn't know what to do around entrepreneurship. That's when I came across a US company called Young Entrepreneurs Academy that had been teaching entrepreneurship to 11–18-year-olds.

Within ten days, I flew over to New Jersey and met the owner—a wonderful lady named Gayle Jagel—and signed the pan-India rights for the academy. Over the course of my six-year journey of working with children, I saw, first hand, the magic that entrepreneurship can work on kids. When you help them come up with a venture that they are passionate about, that solves a problem which is personal to them, they get transformed from nonchalant teens to these balls of energy, ready to conquer the world! We worked with them on prototypes, helped them master the three-minute pitch, generate sales and get funding at *Shark Tank India*-style investor panels. I then exited the US franchise and rebranded the academy as Thapar Entrepreneurs Academy so that I could extend these courses to adults in addition to 11–18-year-olds. I approached the makers of *Shark Tank India* to persuade them that some of my students be given an opportunity to appear on the show. The meeting ended with them asking me if I would like to be a Shark?!

Amid working towards a potential IPO, while dealing with a pandemic and a brutal 10th grade ICSE exam for my older one, saying 'Yes' to *Shark Tank India* wasn't an easy decision. I accepted for one and one purpose only . . . to extend my support to an important cause—celebrating the entrepreneurs of our country!

I wasn't sure if the shoot would be easy. I am used to managing my own schedule, moving between offices and meetings. Here, I was expected to be at a studio in Film City for fourteen hours a day every single weekend for two months!

Three things made this an energizing as opposed to an energy-depleting experience:

1. **The entrepreneurs**: There were days when I would walk in tired as I had not slept enough due to work and personal calls post the fourteen-hour shoots. But the minute these founders walked in, all bright-eyed, high on energy and with big smiles, I was filled with optimism and energy. With their passion, drive and positivity, they wowed us. They inspired us, they moved us and brought tears to our eyes. Overall, it's fair to say that they taught us a lot more than we taught them!

2. **The team behind the scenes**: I had walked in with biases that the media world would not be efficient and that I was used to a certain professional work ethic and discipline at the workplace. I couldn't have been more wrong. Right from the briefing notes to the scheduling to editing, the team has blown me away with their competence, hard work and sincerity towards the cause. For the cynics, I would like to clearly state this and repeat it once more—nothing was scripted. We knew absolutely nothing about the ventures till they walked in that door and pitched to us.

3. **My co–Sharks**: (I didn't know any of them before the shoot). They are super smart and super fun people. On screen we fought for deals but backstage, we danced, laughed and learned a lot from each other. Let's not kid ourselves—when you put five Type A personalities in a room together, there are bound to be disagreements and I have had my

fair share of them. But in the end, we all respected each other, and the cause, enough to let go quickly and look at the bigger picture. Most of us collaborated and co-invested on deals (quite different from other *Shark Tank India* shows across the globe). This, I am sure, will add a lot of value to the founders we have invested in.

I heard some big names from the startup ecosystem criticize the show and say they are happy they said 'No' when they got an offer to be Sharks. All I would like to say is, 'Buddy, you lost a huge opportunity to impact and influence the masses of our country to respect and take on the entrepreneurial route.'

Are there some parts of the show that need improvement? Yes, there are, but it's only Season 1 vs Season 13 in other countries (*Shark Tank India* USA), so stop judging . . . it was new for all of us. We learnt along the way and are still internalizing and evolving. As long as we did this for the right reasons and the right causes . . .

It's not easy to step out of your comfort zone and put yourself in the public eye just for supporting a cause. It's not easy to put in fourteen-hours-a-day shoots and stay away from your family for several weekends in a row. It's not easy to stay thick-skinned when you are being brutally and mercilessly trolled. But can you stay true to your conviction, keep reminding yourself why you took this up and continue to stay authentic? *Shark Tank India* tested every ounce of my inner strength both during the shoot and when the show was aired!

I learned that it is always important to stay kind and grounded; to invest only if you believe in the cause and can add value; to stay humble and keep learning. Did I make my share of mistakes and judgement errors? At times, did I play it safe rather than take risky bets? Of course, I did. But as we evolve as leaders, it's important to learn to show our vulnerability, accept our regrets graciously and keep improving and growing.

The entire shoot ended by 12 December 2021 and the show was launched on 20 December. I sat through around 170 pitches and invested in twenty-five companies that touched my heart. I funded amazing ventures and I know that it's going to be one hell of a fun journey with these crazy mavericks. Mavericks who dared to forge their own path or took the path less travelled as Robert Frost says in his poem, *The Road Not Taken*. It is truly an honour to be a small part of their big vision, to support our nation builders. I will always be grateful to this show for connecting me to these wonderful people who have touched my heart and reminded me about the power of simplicity, ambition and goodness that still exists in our country.

Finally, *Shark Tank India* inspired me to write. There were so many invitations post the show, to speak, to write, and to coach that I felt a book with my thoughts, stories and learnings was something that people would benefit from. This book has a few key lessons that shaped me. I have tried to put in as many stories as possible to make it more relatable. I hope this book inspires and imparts lessons that I have been privileged to learn over the years.

Chapter 2

My Investment Framework

All investors need absolute clarity of thought in terms of what companies they would like to invest in. This ensures they pick the right deals that are a win-win for both the founder and the investor. How will I measure my success as an investor? Neither by the feedback on *Shark Tank India*, nor by the amount of funds invested or even the deals that I won from other Sharks. Rather, the glory will come from two metrics alone: one, if my founders scale as a function of my support and two, if they speak highly of their experience with me as an investor!

Detailed below are the 4Fs of my Funding Framework:

1. **Founder**: I should see that fire in the belly, the drive, sincerity and humility in the founders and feel excited about being part of their journey. As an investor, you are always betting on the person.

2. **Foundation**: They should be solving a deep-rooted problem. I prefer not to invest in prototype or

pre-revenue ventures. I prefer companies that have at least INR 1–2 crore in annual sales so that they have established credibility and gained customer insights. Founders who have had their share of hard knocks while launching their business will rarely fumble when asked questions. They will always be on top of their numbers. I always look for businesses that have a **moat**—a sustainable competitive advantage, which is mostly when the product or service has a unique selling proposition (**USP**). This differentiates them from the rest and ensures that the business will be scalable and profitable.

3. **Financials:** I look for founders who believe in fundamentals of cash flow v/s cash burn. For sure, during the growth phase, there is a time period when profitability takes a hit, but the founder must be able to demonstrate a clear path to profitability with specific milestones and a robust action plan.

4. **Fit:** The venture should fit my expertise and personality as an investor. I should be able to add value. I should be able to help in terms of my expertise in manufacturing, global distribution, marketing and finance. I should feel the founder can benefit from my network in terms of investors (for future fundraise) and business leaders across diverse industries who can collaborate with founders of my portfolio companies.

Of course, I have a special interest in healthcare deals and ventures with women founders. That is no secret.

I would like to elaborate a bit more on 'Expertise' that I have mentioned above. It is a word that I used on the show quite often and became the focal point of the memes created around the show as well. There is a strong mental model proposed by none other than investment guru Warren Buffet called the **Circle of Competence**. Buffet advocates limiting one's financial investments to areas where an individual may have limited understanding or experience and rather, concentrate on areas that one has the greatest familiarity with. Of course, our circle of competence can be widened, but it can only be done slowly, selectively and over time!

In his 1996 letter to Berkshire Hathaway, Buffet further explained, 'What an investor needs is the ability to correctly evaluate selected businesses. Note that word— selected—you don't have to be an expert on every company or even many. You only have to be able to evaluate companies within your circle of competence. The size of that circle is not very important; knowing its boundaries, however, is vital.'

Bottom line, never be afraid to say, 'I don't know!'

Since I had a very clear framework combined with a strong gut instinct, I knew within five minutes whether I wanted to invest in the deal or not. This backfired at times as I was always the first person to say, 'I am out.' To me, it signified clarity of thought; I knew exactly what I wanted and was smart and selective. But, of course, my attitude was easily misconstrued by many as that of someone who didn't want to invest at all, giving rise to a plethora of memes around that! Anyway, I was happy, as I didn't suffer from any regrets on any of the deals I made. The ones that didn't go through were driven entirely by the seller's remorse over **valuation.**

Deals with causes that touched my heart included:

- Altor Helmet (a smart helmet that helps avoid accidents, reports them and gives a driving risk score to its users)
- Thinker Bell (a teaching aid/device for the visually impaired)
- AAS Vidyalaya (a tech platform for increasing literacy rates among 6th to 10th graders)
- Brainwired (a device and app that helps farmers manage the health of their livestock)
- Rare Planet (a platform that promotes Indian handicrafts)
- Watt Technologies (a supersmart teen who wants to keep innovating and solving problems)
- Kabaddi Adda (a platform that promotes the Indian sport kabaddi)

Deals where my expertise, specifically in healthcare, would help, were:

- Menstrupedia (breaking taboos around periods which can be expanded to other women's health issues that need to be addressed)
- The Renal Project (making dialysis affordable in tier-2 and -3 cities)
- Spandan (a portable home care ECG device that can screen for heart ailments)
- Beyond Water (premium water enhancer fortified with vitamins and electrolytes)
- Tagz (healthy snacking options)
- Colour Me Mad (insoles to help with foot problems)

Deals that involved fun products where my networks would help scale include:

- Auli (luxury skincare)
- Skippi (cool icepops)
- Wakao (jackfruit-based non-meat food alternative)
- Nuutjob (male intimate hygiene products)
- Bummer (innerwear brand)
- Nomad (gourmet food spreads)
- In a Can (canned cocktails)
- Find Your Kicks (sneaker reseller platform)
- Storage Company (a pan-India storage service)
- Cocofit (coconut concentrate franchise)
- Sneakare (sneaker storage and accessories)
- Farda (streetwear brand)

Skippi took me back to my childhood and memories of eating popsicles at school. Auli tapped into my love for skincare products. Find Your Kicks is personal as I have three sneakerheads at home carrying back way too many shoes from trips abroad. Bummer takes a category that is often boring and functional and adds an element of in-your-face brashness and quirkiness!

For all my deals, I don't plan on being a passive investor. I want to be their mentor, their sounding board; help them with my business acumen and networks, celebrate their journeys and help them scale. This comes by having a long-term outlook. If the goal is to flip your stake in the next round of funding and make a quick monetary gain, that's one way to look at it, but that's definitely not my way. The mentorship and coaching way requires long-term vision and the conviction to stick with them through thick and thin.

Did I miss any opportunities to invest? Do I have any regrets? Here, I would like to start by saying that as future leaders, we need to champion not just founders who can scale and make money for us but also founders who have tremendous potential and are working on a real problem. They may just not have got the right mentorship to gain traction in their business. Jugaadu Kamlesh and Pandurang Taware of Agro Tourism are both Maharashtrian farmers out to solve real problems but hadn't made sales due to lack of right guidance. We need to be bold and back such founders to ensure they become successful. Entrepreneurship shouldn't just remain the dream of the ones with the right education and resources but also an ambition of the common man. This is one of our core responsibilities as business leaders who have been blessed with power and privilege and who people look up to. Not investing in Kamlesh and Pandurang remains one of my biggest regrets at *Shark Tank India*! I made up for one of the regrets by investing in Pandurang's agri-tourism company post the show.

As John Ruskin says, 'The highest reward for man's toil is not what he gets for it, but what he becomes by it.' I hope I have become a stronger and more evolved investor thanks to this gratifying and memorable experience at *Shark Tank India*!

An Interview with Ace Investor Sanjeev Bikhchandani, Co-Founder, Info Edge

Every founder needs to raise funds at some point in their journey. Learning how an investor thinks and what they are looking for is important to pick the right partner and prepare for a long and productive journey together. Chapter 2 covers some investment mantras that I personally look at while investing but these have been largely influenced by an investor I deeply admire, Padma Shri Sanjeev Bikhchandani. I met Sanjeev six years ago, when I started my entrepreneurship academy. I cold-called him, met him at his Noida office and was blown away, not just by his concise and razor-sharp talk but also by his humility and simplicity! His advice about picking founders from humble backgrounds—people whom the masses can relate to—has been my guiding principle.

'Write stories which will inspire young people from regular middle-class families to dream big and achieve great things. Research the stories. Your takeaways should emerge from the stories and not vice versa,' he guided me when I spoke to him about this book. Always ready to make time for conversations, Sanjeev continues to be a mentor to many like me.

Below are excerpts from a free-wheeling conversation with Sanjeev to understand his investment philosophy and style.

Namita: Sanjeev, you are one of the most sought-after investors today, thanks to your track record. Most questions that I will ask you here are with the intention of helping our readers understand how an investor thinks, what they look for in a founder and venture. Let's start with the basics. How many investments do you make per year and how large is your team? How do you divide time between

your entrepreneurial ventures and your role as an investor?

Sanjeev: We have an outstanding Co-promoter and CEO, Hitesh Oberoi, who leads our operating businesses—Naukri, Jeevansathi, 99 Acres and Shiksha. I am an Executive Director on the board and provide strategic inputs whenever asked. In terms of my role as an investor, I have a very competent team of ten members who evaluate close to a thousand investment proposals per quarter. We end up investing in two or three. We have a portfolio of around forty-five companies and like to be selective. The team is capable of assisting founders on 90 per cent of their requirements in areas like hiring, scaling, fundraising, marketing and technology inputs. But when a founder wants to meet me, I am always happy to mentor and be a sounding board. I suggest but never impose my views. Great founders have a mind of their own. They will talk to you but will not always do what you suggest. As an investor, you should be willing to live with that—nobody becomes an entrepreneur because they are looking for a new boss. You must also understand and accept that you could be wrong. I had advised Deepinder (Zomato) to not go international. They didn't listen—I was proved right. I also advised them to not get into food delivery. Again, they did not listen and I was proved wrong—food delivery is what saved the company during COVID.

Namita: One aspect that stands out for you or sets you apart as an investor is how you have personally held

yourself to the highest governance standards. As a rule, you do not make any investments in a personal capacity. You only invest through Info Edge. Can you tell us your thinking around that? It's truly incredible but how do you maintain this discipline and what is your rationale?

Sanjeev: I am a strong believer in the mantra that if you are winning, ensure everybody wins. I owe my first and foremost responsibility to creating wealth for Info Edge and its shareholders (of whom I am one). I remember when I was asked to join MakeMyTrip as a board member when it was private, I got stock options. To align my interests with Info Edge shareholders, I transferred those ESOPs to Info Edge. A marquee investor from New York called me to understand why I would do this and I said that if I am giving my time to something other than Info Edge then Info Edge must benefit in some capacity from it.

Namita: That is truly exemplary! Coming back to your role as an investor, what sectors do you look to invest in? Are there certain sectors you stay away from?

Sanjeev: We don't invest top down. We believe bottom up is better. We like to meet companies and founders and see what is interesting. If we had a sector first approach, we would never have invested in Zomato or PolicyBazaar because these companies were pioneers and created sectors that did not exist earlier. In general, we invest in technology, internet and mobile app companies, businesses that focus on IP, network effects, where there is innovation, first mover advantage and a chance of getting to market leadership. This naturally results in high operating leverage and high gross margins. We stay away from high capital consumptive businesses.

Namita: Everyone knows about your success with big ventures like Zomato and PolicyBazaar. Can you tell us about two or three other stories where you have been upbeat about investments and what about these stories made you want to invest? This will give our readers good insights into your thinking as an investor.

Sanjeev: What sparks my attention the most is if the founder has grasped a pain point, has personally experienced it and has a solution around it.

In case of Deepinder, it was his experience as a consultant at Bain Capital—waiting in the office cafeteria line, studying the menu and then again, waiting for delivery of his order—that prompted him to scan the menus and put them up on his page on the company intranet. When he was approached on why 95 per cent of the company traffic was getting diverted to his page, he realized that he was solving a real problem.

In case of Yashish of PolicyBazaar, his father was duped by insurance agents. He demonstrated to me how I was paying 60 per cent more than I needed to. Again, a real unaddressed need he was out to solve.

Let me tell you about three other investments of ours. There is a company called Bijnis—the three founders are from Agra. If you look at their CVs or hear them pitch, they will not wow you right away. But what we saw was the fact that they had solid business acumen and a background in manufacturing. Bijnis is basically a B2B platform that has a compelling proposition in the footwear, fashion and lifestyle categories. As an example, the footwear industry has lakhs of small shops and many manufacturers. There is a chain of intermediaries that eat away 40–45 per cent through commissions. It is an imperfect, fragmented and inefficient industry structure that they are trying to solve through their B2B interface. This interface is trying to organize and give a platform to small, unknown brands pan India. They had the first mover advantage. We were an early investor, did two rounds. Now, several blue-chip investors have followed suit.

Another company where we were early investors is Gramophone. These three engineers from IIT Kharagpur, who were part of the agri programme at IIM Ahmedabad, decided to start something as simple as a phone line to solve farmer issues at a gram (village) level for free. When they established credibility and had a large number of farmers approaching them, they went on to build their website and app where farmers can get unbiased advice around multiple areas. In addition to advice, this app also sells inputs to ensure quality and non-spurious products of the highest quality to farmers. Here is a team working out of Indore that has domain expertise and is solving something for Bharat, that is exciting.

Then there are two ventures helping kirana stores pan India. They are working towards making local kiranas financially viable and helping them compete better with e-commerce and organized retail. One is ShopKirana—again, three founders, with a P&G supply chain background. Their goal is to help kirana owners with their supply chain. Currently, a kirana owner has to buy from a wholesaler in bulk and block his cash flow. Instead, he can order just in time from ShopKirana which has an app with a catalog backed by a warehouse and delivery system to manage this. Similarly, 1K Kirana Bazaar is a venture where three founders are solving for tier-3, -4 and -5 cities by helping kirana stores manage their billing, giving them advice through AI on what to stock, and helping them with supply issues. Have you heard of a small town called Dharuhera which is enroute from Delhi to Jaipur? It has a population of 50,000 but has five of these stores. Imagine the enormous potential of kirana stores in our country—the real Bharat as we call it—and here are entrepreneurs who are out to solve real problems that these store owners face.

It excites me to be a part of such journeys where real problems are being solved, where the founders have domain expertise and first mover advantage. Very often, these companies that approach us are pre-revenue or low revenue. We try to understand the founders, their personal journeys, problems they are out to solve and then, at the end of the day, it's a judgement call. Some work out, some don't.

Namita: Do you think being an entrepreneur helps you become a better investor? What are your views on Founder CEO vs Professional CEO?

Sanjeev: Being entrepreneurs and business operators definitely helps us understand operational challenges faced by a founder. We understand their challenges as we have built products and businesses ourselves. We understand the lonely journey of entrepreneurs, the risks, pressures and so, we are more empathetic. We are in it for a much longer horizon than most other investors. This is not to say that an investor without operational experience doesn't add value. These investors may have other strengths they bring to the table such as networks with global companies especially in the Silicon Valley, more access to capital, etc. Regarding CEOs, we feel very strongly about the founder being the CEO as they bring passion, market understanding and long-term thinking like no other. We bet on founders.

Namita: You have invested in two successful companies that recently went public. Lately, investors have become wary of new-age companies. How do

you go about thinking about long-term prospects of these ventures?

Sanjeev: Investors must focus on fundamentals in these companies just like they do in others with key metrics being growth, margin, path to profitability, market share and customer satisfaction. These ventures must start making profits 2–3 years after going public to build investor confidence.

* * *

Sanjeev is a long-term investor and his glory comes from his founders doing well and speaking highly of the support provided by him. He sums it up beautifully when he says, 'You must understand that you are only betting a part of your money while the entrepreneur is betting their life. An entrepreneur bets everything and you have to respect that.'

Chapter 3

Perfect Your Pitch

'You never get a second chance to make a first impression.' This is one of the most brilliant quotes I have come across and it is absolutely relevant for this chapter. The founder gets limited time with investors and they have to plan, practice and make that unforgettable first impression. While 'substance over style' is definitely true—substance is paramount—the magic and impact of the right style cannot be discounted in today's world. Especially when attention spans are short and there is a clutter vying for that limited attention! At *Shark Tank India*, the Sharks saw 8–9 pitches per day, each with an average time span of an hour per pitch (the edited 10–12-minute version is shown on television). It was important for pitchers to have the pitch concise yet interesting enough to not only hold our attention but also walk away with a deal!

As I mull over all 198 pitches and the sixty-two that walked away with funding, there are several commonalities that stand out among those that finally got funded. So, here are few key ingredients that make a perfect pitch:

1. **Solve a deep-rooted problem**: Investors want to understand the purpose and scalability of the venture. The founder should be able to clearly articulate the problem and specifically state the Target Audience Market **(TAM)** that is impacted by the problem. For example, since I am from healthcare and understand the affordability and accessibility gap in our country, The Renal Project (affordable dialysis service) and Spandan of Sunfox Technologies (portable low-cost ECG) appealed to me as both are out to solve for these important problems. Both had a great handle on the statistics and spoke passionately about wanting to make a difference.

2. **Narrate your personal journey**: This is the most important success mantra. A founder must nail this part! Investors ultimately invest in the person; they make a bet on their vision and for that, their personal journey must touch investor hearts. Educational background, family, who inspired them or what incident in their life inspired them to take up this journey, setbacks and learnings along the way. The investors must be able to understand and feel this emotional connect. Passion and conviction should shine through their eyes when the founder is speaking. When Jayanthi Bhattacharya spoke about how her hemp products came about due to her sister's illness and painful journey, it showed us how important this venture was for her as a cause.

Likewise, for Pandurang Taware of Agro Tourism, he had been at this mission of helping farmers for the past sixteen years. He is a farmer himself and understands the importance of showcasing the cultural diversity of rural India and, in the process, helps farmers augment their income. He has won so many awards and worked with the government on important policy changes. Though I didn't invest on his venture at the Tank, his personal journey and persistence stayed with me. I approached him after the show and am thrilled to be investing in his venture.

3. **Know your numbers**: Now this one is a non-negotiable. Just like understanding emotions is important, understanding numbers and the business plan is equally important for investors. A good founder must be so hands-on that basics like selling price, gross margin, **SKUs, shelf life, sales mix**, etc., must be answered with absolute clarity. They must also be able to answer questions around customer insights and competition and their differentiator in a convincing manner. Fumbling around these basics or not having the right numbers in the head shows lack of thoroughness and attention to detail. By far, the most important number a founder has to get right is the valuation they ask for. We saw good businesses that got rejected as the founder asked for unreasonable and often beyond ridiculous valuations. Investors want to know that this has been thought through well. Here, the example that comes to mind is the venture with healthy chips

and dips, #Tagz. I lost to Ashneer but I was super impressed by the founders' grasp on their business basics. Often, things happen too quickly at the Tank and post the show, you get more time to think through the venture. I approached the #Tagz team after the show ended and invested in them. I was absolutely right. Their due diligence was the most efficient and quickest due to their sheer grasp and preparedness where their numbers and accounts were concerned.

4. **Stage of business**: At *Shark Tank India*, **prototype stage** businesses did not get much interest from the Sharks. The post prototype yet pre-revenue businesses were interesting but then again, there was always the lingering doubt that the product–market fit had not been proved through a launch and consumer insights were still missing. The winners were the ones who had launched and had seen reasonable sales to get investors intrigued. They could show a clear path to scale and profitability. I passed on interesting deals like Good Good Piggy and Sabji Kothi as they were only in the prototype stage but Brainwired was one company where I made an exception. Firstly, their journey touched me. They lost their cow, Gauri, who they were very attached to and the doctor's words stayed with them—had they detected her illness early, Gauri could have been saved. This inspired them to launch their AI-enabled livestock health monitoring system. They did not have any revenue but they had firm orders from various state governments and

private organizations and I had the confidence that they would implement and deliver.

5. **Touch and feel the product/technology**: Avid *Shark Tank India* watchers must have witnessed the delight with which we ate all the goodies that were served to us by food business entrepreneurs! Nothing gets Sharks to truly grasp the business more than trying out the product—whether it was tasting the food, feeling the fabric of fashion wear products, checking out the packaging, logo design, using skincare products, trying out the shoes, etc. It was also important to check the simplicity and style of the user interface of their technology, their app and website. Some of you will remember Aman and Anupam trying electric two-wheelers of Revamp Moto and Vineeta zipping around in the EV from Booz. The ability to try and test the products gave a different kind of confidence and connect with the venture.

6. **Stay open to feedback**: This is one of the most important points investors look at. When we invest in an entrepreneur, it's going to be a long journey and we want to be associated with people who are humble, hungry to learn and open to feedback. Very often, we saw Sharks loving the venture, getting impressed by the financials but passing on a deal just because they didn't like the founder's attitude and found them too defensive with mindblocks when it came to listening to Sharks' suggestions. When Aishwarya Biswas of Auli felt she didn't need a co-founder, many Sharks passed on the

deal assuming that she would be a founder who would not be open to new thinking. But I invested in her as I felt that she had gladly accepted a few other suggestions on marketing and finance when we had pointed those out to her. Different Sharks, different styles, and different perspectives on the same founder.

7. **Master your negotiation style**: When Sharks offer a valuation, they fully expect the founders to counter offer. But it's the manner of the counter offer and how they negotiate is what offers priceless insights into the founder's mind. Often, founders were adamant and didn't budge from their valuations, and sometimes, the Sharks caved in. Some Sharks let the deal go. Often, it seemed that the founder was open but some mentor or advisor was quoted as not allowing the valuation. This was a put-off and made several Sharks sense that the founders lacked independent thinking. Bummer and Thinkerbell are great examples. Sulay and Sanskriti didn't budge on the valuation as they were very clear that they would not down-value their respective start-ups compared to what they had raised in their previous round of investment. Such clarity of thought is impressive, even if it means staying adamant on that last 0.1 per cent in the negotiation round. Here are a couple of tips around negotiation: where there is a prior investor, founders can be firm and not down-value at the Tank, citing the anti-dilutive clause in the shareholder agreement. Where there is no prior investor, the founder can use the multiple

commanded by a similar type of company that has fundraised to peg their own range for valuation.

8. **Create a splash**: The drama quotient, what they wore, use of the right props, displays, use of short films, dance and music to convey the essence of the venture was done effectively by many founders! The Sharks just loved this and our faces would light up. The pitch has to be concise but the enthusiasm and energy must be contagious. Animated faces and energetic body gestures are ways to keep Sharks engaged. Humour is a great tool and makes you more likeable and memorable. Beyond Snacks did this incredibly well. He walked in and enacted 'Greasy Anna' in his red lungi to show the unhygienic conditions in which most banana chips are made. Then he tore his black T-shirt to reveal a yellow T-shirt with the Beyond Snacks logo (a perfect colour match with his chips packaging) and brought in a Kathakali dancer in an elaborate costume to serve chips to us! It was the same with the Nuutjob girls who walked in dressed as men with beards and the whole shebang, itching their private parts to demonstrate the need for male intimate hygiene products! Now this is drama and creating a splash.

All these stories are from *Shark Tank India* Season One. *Shark Tank India* not only gave founders an opportunity to present to Sharks and get funding but also the platform to showcase their venture to millions of viewers globally. This is a once-in-a-lifetime opportunity to market your brands. We've heard of websites crashing and founders facing stockouts within hours of their episode airing. Such is the magic of *Shark Tank India*, a unique platform that must be optimized by perfecting one's pitch.

The lessons here have *Shark Tank India* references to make it easy for everyone to relate to them. However, these insights are relevant for all entrepreneurs. It is important to take a step back and internalize that there is a whole world of investors and a fabulous start-up ecosystem awaiting all these bold and driven founders. They are excited to partner with them and invest in them. Hopefully, what I have shared in this chapter, will prepare entrepreneurs for this exciting world and bring a smile on their face, confidence in their hearts and spring in their step as they get on stage to face the bright lights shining on them.

Chapter 4

You've Got the Deal, What Next?

Getting investors interested in your deal post the pitch is just the beginning. The verbal commitment and handshake is like the *'roka'* (in-principle agreement) in Indian marriages. This is followed by a formal engagement called term sheet. Then begins the long courtship of due diligence finally culminating in a partnership that is solemnized by a shareholder's agreement. After that, like all relationships, you have to keep working at it. Both the founder and investor have to be committed.

Listed below are a few pointers for founders in terms of preparatory work and what they can expect post the deal:

1. **Nuances of a term sheet**: A term sheet is typically a summarized understanding of rules governing the relationship. Key points include investor rights, core terms of the deal in terms of capital, equity share, rights of the founders, conditions that must

be fulfilled by the founder prior to the deal and after the deal, among others.

2. **Due diligence**: The investor hires a third party to conduct a detailed investigation that involves checking audited financials, legal paperwork and also background checks. This can take anywhere from three weeks to three months depending on the preparedness of the investee company and the level of details expected by the investor. Often, if the company already has a prior investor and a recent due diligence report is available, that largely expedites the process. Deals fall through in this phase due to lack of transparency or discrepancy in facts provided during the pitch v/s reality. This is where founders need to invest in the right team and consultants to keep their records absolutely updated and organized. This is a reflection of their seriousness and commitment to systems and processes.

3. **Shareholder agreement**: This is the final document that defines **founder lock in**, board or observer seat, **reserved matters**, information rights, **drag** and **tag rights**, exit clause, detailed conditions precedent and subsequent to the deal, **representations and warranties** and **indemnification**. These legal terms are very important and all founders must get a good understanding of these clauses. At the Tank, we were able to close deals quickly with founders who were aware of these terms and negotiations. In case of those who weren't aware, the matter was compounded by advisers who overcomplicated things and confused founders rather than helping

them, delaying deals beyond reasonable time limits.

4. **Secretarial process**: The shareholder agreement is followed by secretarial compliances after which the appropriate share certificate is issued, depending on whether the investor is getting equity or preferred sources like compulsory convertible preference shares or I safe notes.

Unfortunately, post pitch, some deals don't even make it to due diligence due to something commonly termed as 'sellers' remorse'. It refers to an emotional reaction of regret post clinching the deal, when the seller feels they are not happy with the valuation. This has been a common phenomenon in all *Shark Tank India* experiences across various countries. In my case, interesting deals like Wakao, Nuutjob and Colour Me Mad didn't go through for this reason. In some cases, we felt more comfortable giving the capital in tranches based on achievement of milestones (something that is fairly standard and common in most start-up deals). But the founders were not on board with this and we amicably parted ways due to this difference in perspective. Historical data has shown that more than one-third of deals don't go through due to seller's remorse or sticky issues of due diligence where there isn't a meeting of minds.

It is important for founders to network with other founders who can also share their experiences and best practices. An informed founder is a joy to work with and sets the tone for future dealings.

Real work begins after all this paperwork is completed. A few angel investors don't believe in a formal review mechanism and have the founders approach them as and when needed. Other investors like me believe in quarterly calls to check up on data and other business needs. It all depends on the personality of the investor, the role they wish to play (passive vs active), the stake they have (small stake vs large stake) and whether they are lead investors or follower investors, etc.

The areas that are addressed in the quarterly review mechanism typically include an update on sales and profit along with a brainstorming on the marketing plan for future quarters, team and other updates. These interactions can become more frequent when the founder needs to do a fundraise and relies on the investor for advice and connections. All in all, a good investor not only provides business acumen but also acts as a well-wisher and sounding board for strategic discussions.

Reviews must not be thought of as policing opportunities or audit type interrogations but as a chance to share experiences to make the company stronger. Always remember that the investor and founder are on the same side.

Examples of How an Investor Contributes Post Deal

Investors have to provide business acumen in areas that are truly their expertise. This may involve help with marketing connects, help with hiring the right team depending on where current gaps are, help with distribution networks, etc. Emcure is present in seventy countries and these global networks are a massive asset to any founder who has aspirations of scaling at an international level. Not just distribution networks but also possible strategic alliances through licensing opportunities with global business partners. The Renal Project is a good example of this. Since Emcure has connects with top nephrologists and hospitals pan India and globally, these connects can add tremendous topline to a start-up that has the fundamentals in place but is looking for networks to scale.

The biggest area a good investor can help with is future fundraising. Investors are a small community and are constantly in touch with each other. They rely on each other for good deals, shared learning, and best practice sharing. At the right stage, investors can get founders connected to the right investors.

Helping with change in product name and packaging is an interesting one that we often saw at the Tank. First impressions and appearances do matter. The product name must have recall value and should be easy to pronounce. Let's discuss a few *Shark Tank India* examples. Sharks wanted to change the name of an energy drink. It was called NOCD (no carbohydrate drink) and was tough to pronounce. The business was in its early stages and the founders agreed to a name change. I remember all of us discussing that the premium skin care brand I had invested in—Auli— sounded like 'Oily'. But after detailed discussions with the founder, Aishwarya, we mutually decided that the benefits of changing the name did not outweigh all the negatives of changing it at that point in the brand's trajectory. Then, there were instances where investors had different views themselves. For example, Booz was a name that Vineeta did not like but Ashneer felt it had good recall value! Ultimately, the founder has to go with their gut instinct. I remember speaking to Sanjeev Bikhchandani on how he came up with the name 'Naukri' and he said that he did not want to opt for the obvious route and decided to pick a Hindi name. What was interesting is that a majority of his friends and well-wishers advised him not to, saying it sounded 'downmarket' and reminded them of the word 'naukar'(house help in Hindi). Sanjeev ultimately went with his gut and is grateful that he did. The name has become a flagbearer and trendsetter of sorts, inspiring many future founders to use similar names for their ventures.

Overall, an investor's job is to suggest and not impose. There will be founders who will listen to investors but do what they feel is right and this is where it gets tricky. Will the investor give the founder the freedom and flexibility to do what they feel is truly right? This is what differentiates a good long-term investor from a not-so-great partner.

This may seem like a lot of advice from an investor's perspective but I have also been on the other side of the table! Emcure has had two sets of prominent private equity (PE) firms as its investors—Blackstone and Bain Capital— and I have worked closely with both of them during due diligence, and during regular reviews and discussions after the deal. At the end of the day, the founder has to run their business, get involved in operations and take important calls. The investor must always be someone who supports and empowers rather than someone who bogs them down with too many demands and dashboards.

Emcure has had its share of setbacks, but the two toughest ones were when Bain Capital was our PE partner. The setback with our manufacturing facility and the fraud case related to our global acquisition could have literally pushed us into bankruptcy and made Bain Capital lose all their money. Such was our fate that both these events occurred around the same time in our journey. Even though their investment cycle/horizon was extended longer than their norm and while there were many who doubted our ability to emerge out of these two situations, the Bain Capital team stood by us and supported us. Even at the time of our discussions around going public, they put our perspectives and our interests before theirs. I have witnessed, first hand, what a good investor can do for a company, how they can support and not stifle. This, my dear friends, makes all the difference.

Chapter 5

Building Winning Teams

Talent wins and good talent is hard to find. This is why most leaders spend a lot of time in recruiting and motivating key talent. 'People first' ... we have heard this so many times, but do we really know what this means and how to go about building these winning teams? In this chapter, I have shared some learnings from Emcure's story as well as my personal experiences. Building extraordinary teams has undoubtedly been one of the single biggest reasons for our ability to scale Emcure to a global pharma major!

Here are a few insights into how winning teams are built:

1) **Get the right co-founder**: The importance of finding the right co-founder cannot be emphasized enough. At *Shark Tank India*, this was a common point of feedback from most Sharks. Depending on the identified gap, the founder was asked to get a technology or marketing co-founder. A co-founder not only brings the right skillset but is also

invested in the growth and success of the business due to equity that they are typically allotted in the venture. The three biggest points to consider here are as follows:

a. How many co-founders are too many? We saw in several *Shark Tank India* pitches that there were a large number of co-founders and this was a concern. Are there too many decision makers and power centres that will create more complications than ease up running of the business?

b. How are roles defined? Here again, in many cases, Sharks were concerned that roles were not clearly defined. In the case of the Alpino Peanut Butter venture, the six co-founders hadn't even named a CEO. When an impromptu poll was taken on who they thought would be the best fit for the role, there was a massive difference of opinion amongst the founders. The product was fantastic; revenue numbers were unbelievable, but if such basics were not discussed and known, it would make any investor nervous, to say the very least.

c. How is deadlock resolved? This is related to the earlier point. Once clear roles are defined, conflict resolution becomes manageable. Debates and differences are candidly voiced, but there is a clear decision maker for every functional area. Another important aspect of this is that the exit clause for all co-founders must be decided and written down in a legal contract upfront. If there is a falling out or the co-founder chooses to leave to pursue something else, how this will be handled in an amicable and least disruptive manner must be clearly defined.

2) **Founder CEO vs professional CEO**: This is one of the toughest questions a start-up faces. Founders bring passion, domain expertise, command respect from employees and are committed to a long-term play. But there are times when a founder can be a bottleneck when the venture scales. Sometimes, they find it difficult to be tough or let go of team members who have been with them from the very beginning, even when they may not be right for the business at that point. They may not be able to adapt to the needs of a venture as it scales, with regard to the level of operational competence, and attention to systems and governance that is essential for a larger and more complex organization. Sometimes, getting a professional CEO is in the best interests of the business and also in the interest of building credibility while raising the next round of funds. This is also important during Mergers and Acquisitions (M&A).

At Emcure, we acquired several companies within India and internationally to help us scale. Every single time, we have retained the founder as the CEO. Their skin in the game, and deep understanding of local markets has always benefitted us. However, trusting someone enough to make them CEO can, at times, backfire too. We have made several global acquisitions and learnt some things the hard way. Retaining the founders and being overdependent on them without adequate checks and balances in place has led to fraud and embezzlement of funds. We have had to fire the founders and face the brunt of lawsuits that followed. My father never lost his trademark optimism even during these rough years. He looked at this as an opportunity to learn. Under his guidance, we ensured that we strengthened our finance and digital controls and additionally, sent our trusted senior leaders from India to those geographies to head key functions. This would ensure stronger corporate governance going forward.

3) **Set the right culture**: In recent times, a lot has been written about the severe skill shortage of tech folks in the start-up ecosystem and measures being taken to hire and retain this talent. Keeping your key talent motivated and ensuring that they keep growing with the organization through challenging work, clearly defined growth paths and stock options is important. Encourage dissent, make it safe to fail and learn. Letting each member shine, feel appreciated and recognized is easier said than done. A good leader always gives credit to the team. **Lao Tzu, the famous Chinese philosopher, rightly said, 'A leader is best when people barely know he exists, when his work is done, his aim fulfilled, they will say: we did it ourselves.'**

Walk the Talk

At Emcure, my father defined the culture by leading from the front. At 71, he works harder than any employee and leads by example. It is a result-oriented culture but with a CEO who is approachable. My father prefers the shop floor to his office, doctors' clinics to board rooms. He loves speaking to his employees, often beginning his speeches in his trademark booming voice and singing his favorite Bollywood song or recounting some cricket fact or story. These gestures build trust and respect, and has pushed teams at Emcure to aspire for more, work harder and stay longer at the company.

Genuine Empathy Works

Very often, we get so caught up in the rat race that we forget to pause, breathe and focus on the mental and physical fitness of our teams. Another trait that I admire about my father is that even when he was a struggling entrepreneur, he always took the time to invest in his fitness and nudged all his team members to do the same. He would actually pay for their membership at gyms and get yoga trainers at the workplace. People never forget the fact that you care enough to not just invest in their careers but also in their personal health. These are the intangibles that motivate and move teams.

Good Corporate Governance

Teams don't merely mean internal hires but also the team of external guides and mentors. My father was way ahead of his time and, from the very beginning, despite running a private company, built a strong team of external board members who were unafraid to ask tough questions when needed and be supportive coaches at other times. Strong teams that ensure corporate governance, whether it is board members, auditors, or tax consultants is what truly differentiates the all-stars from the also-ran.

Dealing with Difficult Times

It is easy to focus on setting the culture when the going is good, but can the leader stay calm, have a long-term vision and not blame their teams when all hell breaks loose? We had two massive setbacks at Emcure around 2015—the fraud in our global subsidiary and the import alert in our USFDA injectible facility. Both these events happened around the same time and I remember two big banks wanted to recall the term loans they had given to Emcure which could have pushed us to bankruptcy. Those were very dark days. But we managed to emerge out of this relatively unscathed. Firstly, we approached multiple banks and are grateful to the senior leadership team of a nationalized bank for believing in us and giving us a massive loan to pay back the two banks who wanted to pull out. For this faith and support during our toughest times, we will always be indebted. Our finance team, supported by my father, (he was part of every call and meeting, and read every word of the loan agreements) really rose to the occasion.

They were proactive and quick in closing this (the loan) so that the manufacturing and technical teams could stop worrying about funds and start working on rebuilding the business. Secondly, the team hired experts and worked hard on bridging gaps in the old manufacturing facility. But, when they realized that this wasn't working, they were quick to build a completely new facility to get required approvals. These were very tough years for the company and resulted in a massive drain on the bottom line as well as our image and credibility. We let go of a few leaders who were not able to handle the crisis and adapt. It was painful as many of them were old-timers and loyalists, but it was needed for the company to evolve and move forward. A good leader must put company before self and personal relationships. This agility in action and solution mindset was possible only due to the fact that instead of playing the blame game, the teams focused on a specific and sustainable action plan and supported each other. A good leader has the ability to build this positive mindset, this collaborative and 'can do' attitude in teams at the toughest of times.

Long Waiting Game

Sometimes, teams don't produce immediate results. For example, in our biotech business, gestation periods are very long. Research to launch can take over ten years in some cases and keeping a highly qualified team motivated through that period requires an entirely different skillset. My father did that very effectively by being patient, long-term focused and ensuring that their KRAs were more effort than outcome-driven. Offering equity was also a highly effective way to retain such talent and keep them motivated.

Organization-First Approach

Being deeply emotionally connected to their business but staying dispassionate enough to make the right and rational decisions in shareholder interest is often a tough balance for a founder. In 2019, we decided to demerge the US business from the rest of our business for various strategic reasons. Emcure would now be two separate companies with different identities and managements and not a single entity. This demerger elicited mixed reactions from many within the company. However, my father stayed firm and kept his eye on the end goal. Eventually, he convinced the team of the benefits of doing so. He didn't let his or his team's emotions, of wanting to stay in their comfort zone and working with a single combined entity, get in the way of doing the right thing. He has, time and again, demonstrated that for him, organizational interest always precedes personal likes and dislikes.

4) **Hiring and firing:** Do you hire for the right degrees, pedigree/resume or take a bet on people?

Skills can be taught but attitude can't. From myriad resumes and interviewees, how do you spot the driven and enthusiastic ones who can be great team players and pick them, even if their resumes show certain gaps in skills? Bottom line, how do you enlist for potential?! Equally important is letting go of employees who are not productive. If an employee has inherent issues like laziness, lack of integrity and arrogance, it is important to let go of them immediately, before they ruin the team spirit and overall culture of the organization.

Emcure is extremely diversified in terms of presence in multiple geographies and product lines. Whenever my father ventured into completely new areas like API and biotech or new geographies, what helped him succeed was his ability to hire the best team of experts. Many have left the company to start their own ventures in the healthcare space. We often joke that Emcure is a CEO factory where we create many entrepreneurs and able competitors from within the organization! He has used generous equity stake and offered titles including CEO to motivate several professionals to helm subsidiaries and build new businesses. It is incredible to see what ownership and empowerment can do to push people to deliver results way beyond expectations.

Even while firing, it's always been a company first approach, always with a professional rationale. It's never personal. That is the reason why so many who we have asked to leave, continue to stay in touch with my father and till today, invite him to important personal functions.

However, not all firings can have pleasant or even neutral outcomes. Tough times call for tough actions to conserve the bottom line and cash flow. Add to that the pressure when commitments are made to external investors, and it makes matters a lot worse. We have always given competent people many opportunities but we haven't always been quick to let go of people who have not shown improvement despite being given several chances. This led to a situation where we had several overstaffed divisions with too many mediocre performers. One of my toughest decisions at Emcure was to do a one-time correction of this hangover by shutting down entire divisions that were not performing, as well as laying off medical representatives who were non-performers. Right from who those people were, the geographies, what additional severance pay we could manage, to the impact on the topline, planning all of it was painful but necessary. Execution was even tougher. I lost two very senior members of the team as they could not handle the pressure. What followed was massive trolling and threats against me on social media. Numerous lawsuits were filed in states that have strong unions of medical representatives. You need nerves of steel to deal with something like this while focusing on business at the same time. The biggest thing that gets you through is knowing that you did this due to your 'organization first' principle. When that is your guiding mantra, no personal pain or stress can distract you from what is really important for the organization.

Time given by founder and CEO to team development: Many CEOs are increasingly devoting more time to this aspect, and really connect with their employees through offsites and various employee engagement platforms. There is an interesting example from Starbucks. They shut down all 7100 stores for a day in February 2008 for training their teams on how to make the perfect espresso. The company lost $6 million in sales and was roasted by all for doing that but the CEO, Howard Schultz, was very clear that this was an investment which was much needed for strengthening the company's culture. Leaders increasingly need to be connected to their teams, visit the shop floor, work with them, and be approachable. They need to know that the leader has their back, will protect them and is invested in their success. A good leader fills employees with a sense of purpose and creates a culture of trust— the two most important intangibles in building teams. These sound so simplistic but are incredibly difficult to implement. Time, discipline and effort need to be dedicated to building teams, nurturing them and empowering them.

After all these years of working with my father at Emcure, do I think my father made a few errors in team building?

Very often, he micro-managed. However, he has always been open to change and got better after we gave him feedback on this. Also, I do believe that at times, he trusted people too much. It's important to empower, but it is equally important to put checks and balances in the system. This becomes even more pertinent, especially as you scale. And this is something we, as a team, slipped up on a couple of occasions and learned the hard way.

Building winning teams isn't a one-time effort but a culture, an ongoing investment and once this is ingrained in the DNA of the organization, the team truly becomes the secret sauce that helps a company endure and survive the toughest of tests and times in its trajectory!

Chapter 6

Building Big Brands

Brands are the essence of any business and brand building is the key to success. Brands are what differentiate your company from your competitors in the customer's mind. They build customer loyalty and, ultimately, your corporate identity. Brands are what get you higher margins and that in turn, gets you the best market valuation.

I am not going to regurgitate the 3Cs and 5Ps of marketing or hand you a Kotler book. I want to tell you what I learned from my work experience of creating and growing brands at Emcure as well as my interactions with Rajiv Bajaj, MD of Bajaj Auto, a leader and a company that I deeply admire for many reasons, specifically for their innovative thinking in marketing and for being true trendsetters in our country.

So, let's look at a few marketing principles to understand what it takes to build large and sustainable brands that outlast you.

1) **How incremental is your differentiator:** Brands are always built in the consumer's mind. What your brand is being perceived as is the key. For a strong perception, one must have a strong differentiator. How significant is this differentiator to entice existing consumers to stick to your brand and make others shift? Is it 10 per cent, 20 per cent, X per cent better? Figuring this out is priceless. This is the intersection at which marketing and science (R&D/engineering) must combine to deliver that differentiator at a cost and price that the company and customer can both afford. Let's look at Bajaj Auto to understand this. There is a specific and logical differentiation metric that they follow for their launches and I have summarized that below:

   a. The customer typically doesn't care for less than 10 per cent differentiation however much the marketing team may get excited by this marginal improvement.

   b. 10–20 per cent differentiation benefits the market leader but not the #2 or challenger brand.

   c. 20–33 per cent differentiation drove the 125 cc Discover brand launch which was a significant differentiator in customers' minds and therefore a big success. That is, till they made the blunder of launching a 100 cc Discover. The launch of the 100 cc changed the perception of Discover from a differentiated brand to a 'me too' brand. As the market leader, Hero had firmly established itself strongly in the minds of customers as the leader of the 100 cc segment.

    d. 33–50 per cent differentiation led to the launch of Bajaj Auto's biggest success story—the 150 cc Pulsar brand, a differentiator strong enough to create a massive brand for them.

    e. Finally, the quest for 50 per cent plus differentiation led to the KTM collaboration and the launch of KTM bikes which have a strong racing brand perception.

2) **What is your novelty factor?:** In mature industries, technologies are saturated and there often isn't a strong differentiator. Here, the key is to play on perception rather than reality. But the perception should be strong, credible and tangible. Brand perception equals product plus story. How can you tell your story such that it breeds desire in the minds of the end user is essential to get right. In many industries such as the fragmented pharmaceutical world of branded generics, you won't always have the luxury of a strong USP. In such a scenario, your ability to highlight your novelty factor in the two minutes you get in the doctor's chamber is what works. We work on innovative in-clinic campaigns that make the reps engage the doctor in the most effective manner. We recently started live case discussions and a formal mentor programme between senior doctors and young doctors. Sometimes, such innovation in user experience is what builds trust and respect for novelty. Similarly, when Bajaj launched its motorcycle, V, from the scrap of the iconic ship, INS *Vikrant*, it instantly created a novelty factor that

didn't require excessive PR. So all in all, it's about making your story around the novelty factor—simple, yet effective and memorable. In summary, products only generate sales but when a product becomes a brand is when you get sustainable profits.

3) *Jo dikhta hai woh bikta hai* (**What you see, sells**): This one sentence has many nuances to it. In many companies that are based on technology, this alludes to ensuring that a product launch appeals to early adopters/mavericks. Others will buy based on this adoption. It is important to remember that people buy what they see others buying and wanting. There is a 'herd mentality'. In pharma, we ensure that doctors who are considered key opinion leaders (KOLs) or thought leaders are convinced of the superiority of our molecule through effective pre-launch focus groups and advisory boards. Once these doctors adopt our brand and are engaged in talking about it at various conferences and medical meetings, we can rest assured that many other followers will start prescribing the brand too. In the consumer world, this mantra translates to brand visibility. This could mean the most effective shelf space, noise levels through the right influencers at a regional and national level, and the right engagement through effective digital mediums.

4) **Narrow your focus**: While we are working on creating differentiation and a novelty factor, we should not get carried away with doing too many things at one time. This is where marketing is counter intuitive. People somehow feel smarter and more important when they do too many things—cluttered

slides, slew of new launches and line extensions to show how complex they are capable of thinking. But here, the key is focus which also means less is more. The hard reality is that at the heart of all brand building is execution rigour and simplicity, which essentially means doing few things with absolute razor-sharp focus. This is beautifully summarized by Michael Porter who said that the essence of strategy is choosing what not to do. My father had once asked Rajiv Bajaj why he didn't feel the need to diversify into four wheelers. His answer was simple—they wanted to focus on motorcycles and become specialists. Sure enough, they have emerged as the world's most valuable two-wheeler company and have earned their tagline—World's Favourite Indian—with over 58 per cent sales from exports to over seventy countries. This focus also helped them adapt to disruptive macro trends by pivoting from being a scooter maker to a single-minded focus on motorbikes to now adapting to electric vehicles. At Emcure, I practised this mantra by reducing new launches to 1–2 per year and by picking two levers for every big brand to make it stronger and bigger. Once these two levers were identified, we executed with precision, monitored, measured and incentivized the field to ensure we met targets.

5) **Always choose excellence over scale**: Scale is always the by-product of focus on excellence. Excellence comes by setting high standards through innovation. This is what gives you your USP, your differentiator. We have often seen players who, in a quest to meet publicly committed delivery timelines, scale in a

hurry. They compromise on depth and excellence required in R&D, manufacturing and pre-testing, often resulting in product failures, recalls and loss of credibility. At Emcure, we focus on research and innovation by identifying molecules through which we can be first to India or then make the molecule superior through lower dosage or lower side effects. For example, most pregnant women detest taking iron due to massive gastric issues. Emcure was the first to launch a novel molecule, ferrous ascorbate, that significantly reduced this side effect. As a result, we are in a dominant position in the 'iron for pregnant women' segment. Since then, we have launched a full range of innovative iron molecules for anaemia at various stages in a woman's lifecycle. Excellence in innovation helped. At Bajaj Auto, the R&D team is 35 per cent of their workforce, a statistic that demonstrates their commitment to excellence. This can be summed up by what Rahul Bajaj told his son, Rajiv, when he joined the family business. 'Do what you think is best but make sure you are the best at what you choose to do.' This is what excellence truly means!

6) **It is better to be first to market than it is to be better:** It is important to point this out as this is a classical mistake made during most brand launches. Often, we try to keep polishing and improvising the product till we get it right. This delay, this quest for perfection, can cost us our first to market entry which can often be the most critical factor for a brand. If the collective wisdom of your team

indicates that your product is innovative and excellent, launch it. Tweaking and improvising based on consumer insights can keep happening through improved versions post launch, but don't delay launches in the quest for perfection. It is cheaper to be wrong (and keep correcting) than to be late to market.

7) **Collaboration:** Often, collaborations are a great way to augment sales and leverage strengths of both partners to build even bigger brands. The typical 'sum of parts is greater than a whole' theory is true for brand building. The pharmaceutical industry, for instance, has done this very effectively. Several Indian companies including Emcure have licensed brands from global companies. The global company has the technology and the Indian company has the reach, penetration and relationships with medical practitioners due to their large field forces, a win-win for all. Emcure is a leader in anaemia management and an exclusive collaboration with Swiss company, Vifor, helped us launch a novel injectible in this space. It not only entrenched our position as a market leader but gave us a larger portfolio when we approached doctors. Bajaj Auto has used collaborations with KTM and Triumph to become a global leader and also to get an edge in the electric vehicle race. Now, its collaboration with start-ups like Yulu, in the shared mobility space, is going to be one to watch out for.

8) **Competition**: Often, your strategy is dictated not by what the consumer wants but what competition

will allow. Bajaj Auto decided their global market strategy i.e., which countries they would enter, based on where their competition was weak. Similarly, Emcure has historically had a regional strength in the western part of India. So, when we pilot projects, whether it is hiring additional field representatives or the partial launch of a new molecule, we always start with the west. After we gain dominance here and the right customer insights, we launch the brand pan India! Another example is when we realized that competition is mostly focused on doctors in their private practice or large hospitals. This left a whole segment unattended—nursing homes—a segment that we decided to focus and double down on. In most industries, there are no virgin markets. So understand your competition really well and then enter and attack where they are weak.

9) **Importance of market research and feedback**: Customer obsession is the key to success for any brand. For this, the importance of market research to gain important consumer insights cannot be discounted! It is important to systematically get these insights through focus groups, surveys and use this feedback to keep reviewing your brands and improving. At Emcure, we meet our key doctors very often for insights. Let me demonstrate how this helped in increasing sales for one of our key brands. Ferrous carboxy maltose, an iron compound, was an innovative drug we brought to India with two SKUs—500 mg and 1000 mg. But 500 mg made

up 80 per cent of our sales, while 1000 mg got in 20 per cent. Through top doctor surveys, we found that 1000 mg was needed more often, given the weight profile of the pregnant women. It was also more economical as women didn't need to come back for a second dose. This one insight from our market research changed the way we started talking about this molecule in our medical literature, in our brand reminders, in the doctor's clinic and in the way we trained our field force. This in turn helped us change our sales mix, increase our market share and double the value of the brand within twelve months.

10) **Marketing for D2C companies:** I would also like to talk about Direct to Consumer (D2C) companies that have gained traction in the past few years, more so during the COVID pandemic. All the mantras mentioned above are so fundamental to good marketing that they are applicable to legacy as well as D2C companies and are essentially industry agnostic. However, there is one interesting difference in the marketing philosophy for D2C brands. This has to do with their approach towards distribution and digitization. Most legacy companies worked with offline distribution and it's only in the last few years that they have invested in digital capabilities for customer engagement and distribution. On the other hand, D2C brands start with digital distribution through various marketplaces and their own websites. They use digital means for customer engagement, be it influencer marketing, building

emotional connect through ads and through search engine optimization tools. **Customer acquisition cost (CAC), average order value (AOV), repeat customers** and **lifetime value of a customer (LTV)** are key parameters to measure and improve. However, D2C brands are also realizing that beyond a point, if they need to scale, they also need strong offline presence. The majority of Indians still shop offline and an omnichannel strategy is what drives scale and success.

All of the above might seem like too many lessons but no matter what insights I offer in this book, ultimately, they are broad guidelines. Nothing teaches marketing better than sitting with your end consumer and R&D team and absorbing, imbibing, and learning till you crack that product-market fit! In summary, you don't always need a marketing or management degree to learn the basics of brand building. In fact, Rajiv Bajaj does not have an MBA degree from a fancy business school. He is a proud engineer who started from the ground up from the shop floor, built big brands like Pulsar by learning from customer insights, by trying and failing and **pivoting**. I would like to summarize this chapter with an interesting perspective from him. He often says that he has learned all his management lessons from yoga and homeopathy, two disciplines that he is passionate about. When asked about brand building, he stresses on the importance of alignment and sums it up beautifully by saying yoga teaches us alignment and the most important trait of a winning brand is alignment. There has to be alignment of vision. This means that everyone from the chairman to the watchman must know the strategy and every single person and resource in the company must be aligned with this strategy and move in the same direction at the same time. This is what makes a winning brand and a winning company!

Chapter 7

Role of Mentors

At *Shark Tank India*, after every pitch, the Sharks would make an offer at a particular valuation. Several pitchers would take a two-minute break to speak to their mentors and seek their guidance on whether to accept the offer or not. In one such pitch, the founder rejected our offer based on his mentor's advice. I remember a discussion that followed between Ashneer, Aman and me on the role of mentors. They showed some of this debate at the end of Episode 19. I was speaking about how mentors have helped me become who I am today and Ashneer countered by saying that he believes that one doesn't need a mentor in life. Is there a right or wrong answer to this? Absolutely not. It's a completely personal choice.

I wanted to share my thoughts on what a mentor means to me and how I am who I am because of my good fortune of having three outstanding mentors.

Picking a Mentor

A mentor is someone who you deeply respect and want to emulate. Sometimes, it could be a domain expert who can guide you. But a mentor need not be from the same industry. Rather, it has to be someone who can inspire you, give you brutally honest feedback at times, and lift your spirits at other times. A mentor need not always be older than you. At times, it can also be a peer. For example, in an entrepreneur's journey, it helps to have successful founders as mentors as they can relate to the struggles and challenges. Their feedback could be more real, practical and contextual.

I have a mentor who is on the board of Emcure and that made it easier to approach him. My other two mentors are folks I didn't know but admired and therefore cold-called and requested that they mentor me. Fortunately for me, both said 'yes'. So look around you, identify the people you look up to and just ask, you may get lucky like me! If not, keep looking and asking. Also, if a mentor doesn't work out the way you had anticipated, like any relationship, a timely exit on good terms is always the best solution.

There have been many inspiring leaders who I have looked up to, but they haven't been able to commit the time to have regular interactions with me. Being a mentor is a commitment of time and energy and it's not an easy role for leaders who are already overwhelmed and preoccupied with their busy professional lives. But it is also the noblest and most gratifying way to give back and help others truly reach their full potential!

A mentor is a teacher best summed up in the words of Khalil Gibran. **'The teacher who is indeed wise does not bid you enter the house of his wisdom but rather leads you to the threshold of your mind.'**

Expectations from a Mentor

I always thought that a mentor would help me think through my business decisions, help me network with the right people, and teach me important management lessons. But boy, was I wrong or what! Fortunately for me, one of my mentors showed me how wrong my expectations were. He helped me understand that what was more important was to strengthen my core, learn to be in touch with my inner voice, get rid of my ego and become a kinder and more authentic person. Once your core is strong, the rest will follow! My long list of three year, five-year and ten-year goals with timelines and milestones got substituted with two life goals—Know Yourself and Help Others. Once you simplify your life, everything else just falls in place. You get the strength to deal with anything, no matter what life throws at you!

Biggest Skill a Mentor Needs to Have

A mentor should be proactive, and observe and discuss areas of improvement that you may not be consciously aware of. They have your best interests at heart and will never judge or exploit your vulnerabilities. Instead they are always looking for ways to help you and your venture grow, either through their expertise, networks or by just being good listeners, at times.

We all lead complex, stressful lives. We need someone with whom we can be our vulnerable selves, someone with whom we need not posture or overthink. Someone we can speak our heart out to. It is the most therapeutic feeling and a mentor allows you to do just that. A mentor is not expected to know the answers and tell you what to do but has the magical powers to ask the right questions that will lead you to your own insights and answers. Sometimes, this could be through a short conversation and sometimes, through quotes or suggestions on books to read!

The Best Payback for a Mentor

I have been fortunate to have fantastic mentors. My mentors have played various roles in my life. They have helped me get better at my work through timely inputs on marketing, strategic calls I have had to make, and even hiring decisions. They have been a sounding board when I have had emotionally trying moments at work, especially when I have had disagreements with my father. They have helped me evolve as a more authentic person, by gently nudging me to be a better listener, to be less judgemental and overall, a calmer person. Most importantly, I have learned to find and trust my inner voice. My biggest desire in life is to now mentor those who may need someone to guide and help them. Do I have the ability to do regular one-on-one sessions? May be with 2–3 mentees, but my writings, my talks, and my edtech academy can help spread the message and teach others what I have learned with age and time and from my mentors. My portfolio companies have gifted me the unique opportunity to be a sounding board and a guide to these driven and passionate founders. I am excited to be a part of their journeys.

Such is the chain of mentorship, that what you receive, you must generously give to others. That is the best payback for a good mentor!

A Conversation with Sahil Barua, Managing Director and CEO, Delhivery

Sahil Barua is an entrepreneur I have known and admired for seven years now. Again, I had cold-called him when I started my entrepreneurship academy. I remember meeting him seven years ago in his Gurugram office. My first impression was that he was one of the most down-to-earth, fun and super smart people I have met. He talks really fast, so you have to focus hard to keep up with his pace of thoughts and words. But then, over the years, I saw how ridiculously generous he is. In spite of having no time, he selflessly contributed to my entrepreneurship academy every single year—as a speaker, as a judge at our investor panel, as a field trip host. He conducted mentoring sessions with our alumni and when he couldn't make it, he would ensure one of his co-founders personally substituted for him. Who does that while building a unicorn at the same time?! But that's Sahil for you!

We have all heard about Delhivery's fantastic business model, scaling through technology, setting new benchmarks and standards in an erstwhile unorganized and highly inefficient industry. Today, we won't repeat all that you can easily read and find on the internet or in books on Delhivery.

I want to delve into the softer, less-spoken aspects. So in this interview, Sahil gives us a sneak peak into three areas that are covered in this book—role of mentors, culture of dissent and women leaders!

Namita: Sahil, let's start with talking about your mentors. How did you find them and what role have they played in your personal and professional life?

Sahil: I have had many mentors but here, let me talk about the four most important individuals who helped us shape Delhivery and contributed to making it what it is today!

The first one is Abhishek Goyal, who was our very first angel investor. Abhishek was Mohit's (one of my co-founders) senior from IIT Kanpur. After a stint at Accel Partners, he was building UrbanTouch at the time. He was pretty well known in the start-up ecosystem as one of the early investors in Flipkart back in the day. We were young entrepreneurs who had no clue about what fundraising entailed. I remember that he made the effort to sit us down and talk to us about fundraising, what it meant and why it was important for us to have an investor on board. He gave us INR 10 lakh in 2011 and the beauty is that he could have taken advantage of our ignorance. But his terms were always fair and in the interest of the founders. He was out to help and not to make a quick buck. Since then, he has introduced us to many start-up founders who went on to become our clients over time. Best of all, Abhishek introduced us to one of our key co-founders, Kapil!

Abhishek also introduced us to a friend who then introduced us to our second mentor, Gautam Sinha. Gautam had taken over as CEO of Times Internet around the same time as we started Delhivery. We met him in 2012, and within an hour of meeting us, he offered to invest a million dollars in the company! With Gautam, it was never just about the money. He was on our board and his simple philosophy has always been, 'I will be on your board for as long as you want me to and I will help you when you ask me to.' He has been such an integral part of our journey. We still have photographs of him at office inaugurations and warehouse poojas. He has really been there for us every step of the way.

One of our hardest times was when we needed to do a rights issue. We ran out of cash because we grew faster than expected and needed working capital desperately. We had something like twenty days of cash left. Some of our investors were sceptical as the markets had tanked, and no bank would have lent us the money in time. This is where unstinted support and blind faith by a mentor comes in. Gautam simply picked up the phone and told all our investors that he was happy to lead the round and put in the entire money if they didn't participate. One call changed everything. All of our investors immediately agreed to subscribe to the issue.

The third set of people who helped us tremendously have been Brij and Suvir from Nexus Venture Partners. They not only took a punt on us as investors early on but also took the time to introduce us to bankers (including Gaurav and Abha from Avendus, who have been our bankers and friends for nearly a decade), lawyers and other investors when we were completely new to all this and didn't know how to go about things. We were always clear on our strategy and how to build the business. But we were completely raw and inexperienced when it came to dealing with multiple stakeholders as we scaled and this is where they helped a lot. Right from hiring advice, to how to deal with different customers to opening doors, they were always a phone call away and no question was too small or insignificant to ask. We asked them about anything and everything.

That is the level of comfort and confidence we had in them. These conversations have given us priceless insights and have always been thought provoking and helped us grow as individuals and as a company.

The fourth mentor who played the most important role in our early days was Anshoo Sharma. Suraj, Mohit and I had worked with Anshoo at Bain. When we started off, we were thinking of ourselves as a purely food delivery play. Anshoo was the one who opened our eyes to the whole e-commerce logistics sector and pushed us to think big, to think about how we could solve problems in this sector. Delhivery developed its vision eventually from this sound advice given by a friend who really cared and wanted to see us succeed.

Namita: Beautiful, heart touching stories. Is there a reason you refer to them as mentors and not networks here?

Sahil: To me, the word networking can imply a transactional and sometimes, short-term kind of relationship. Our mentors are people who have invested their time and energy in us, and have been a part of our journey for years. Sure, some of them have been financially invested in us but what they have done for us is often way beyond the call of duty. The beauty of good mentors is that they don't wait for you to approach them and ask for help. Often, they watch you and proactively suggest things you need to do differently.

To demonstrate this, I want to talk about two women mentors we have been fortunate to have. One is Renuka Ramnath of Multiples. Renuka was on the board of Air India, at the time. One day, she simply called us and asked us why we weren't working with Air India for air logistics. Then, she went out of her way to connect us to the concerned person there. More recently, even a few years after Multiples had exited as an investor, she spent time guiding us on how to build the company's board and recommended us to some of our current directors. She went out of her way to be a supporter of Delhivery. We were lucky to have another superb board member in Hanne Sorensen. A few months after joining our board, Hanne told me quite succinctly that she had been observing me for four months and felt that I wasn't communicating effectively enough with our team. I didn't get it initially, as I felt that I was having regular meetings with the core team, but she explained that I needed to be out there communicating more through team meetings and field visits. Also that sometimes, if I had nothing to talk about, I needed to simply listen more. We took this to heart as a team, and put it in practice most during all the early days of COVID, when we ran daily 4 p.m. town halls for nearly seventy-five days straight. Those months gave our team the confidence and security to enable the company to grow massively in both years! I personally believe that as we have moved from a team of eight employees to now 80,000, this lesson in communication has been one of the pillars that has helped us operate better.

Namita: Since we are talking about women, I want to touch upon the unique work you are doing in getting more women on your rolls?

Sahil: We all feel very strongly about this. Women are 50 per cent of our population and need more representation in the workforce. Our first aim is to have the highest percentage of women in the logistics industry. It isn't that women aren't willing to join this sector; it's just that companies haven't made enough effort to make changes to the work environment to make it more women-friendly. Just in operations alone, by improving facility infrastructure (something as simple as better toilets, which we should have had anyway), providing transportation and thirdly, by ensuring safety, we have been able to hire a much larger number of women.

Namita: Let's talk about another area that I am passionate about and that you have beautifully harnessed in your company—the culture of dissent?

Sahil: We are five co-founders. Suraj, Mohit and I met while consulting at Bain. Kapil was introduced through Abhishek. We were introduced by a common friend to Bhavesh (at the Hard Rock Café in Mumbai at 12.30 a.m. when we were quite buzzed). I called him nearly three years later and we asked him to join, an offer which he happily took us up on. All of us are strong personalities and disagree a lot. We are used to articulating our points clearly and usually with sound reasoning. The hope is that this reinforces to new team members that dissent is an important part of our culture. There is a big reason why (I think) this is particularly important in the start-up space. Often, since speed is a premium, in our quest of moving with urgency, we take the first approach/first solution or decision that comes to our mind and then focus more on execution. In our meetings, we try our best to challenge opinions, present opposing points of view, and ask many 'what if' questions to push our operating teams to really think hard of gaps and potential pitfalls of any decisions. This has become so ingrained in our culture that there is a running joke that if you have to meet Kapil, you better walk in with four plans for any problem as he will challenge every word that comes out of you. Many have labelled this as 'an aggressive culture' and advised us to 'tone it down a bit' but all of us strongly believe that this is what helps us make the best decisions and this is here to stay!

Namita: With 80,000 employees, how do you ensure these common set of values such as dissent and others are clear to everybody across the board?

Sahil: It is really very simple. Delhivery is a very hands-on company. There is no substitute to being visible and on the field. We don't believe in sitting in our offices and managing by remote control. You will never find our management team simply holed up in a board room. Our meetings are more likely to happen in our warehouse in Bilaspur! This is also a part of our interview process, especially for senior hires where a facility visit pre-interview is a must to really understand their thinking and approach. The entire senior team is aligned with our vision and the entire team is constantly on the ground, on the field, meeting and visiting our employees, our customers and this is the only way to build a winning culture and a winning team!

Chapter 8

Importance of Culture of Dissent

I am a big supporter of dissent which means disagreement and debate. In fact, at Emcure, I have deliberately and carefully cultivated the culture of dissent in my team. We expect leaders to speak up, give contrary views and challenge each other as we truly believe that the best decisions emerge from such spirited debates.

As a culture, Indians are not too comfortable with dissent. Dissent leads to confrontation, unpleasantness, and people holding grudges. Herd mentality, group think and agreeing with the majority are easier, and make us seem more popular. This is mainly due to years of childhood conditioning where many of us have memories of arguing, disagreeing, asking too many questions and quickly being labelled as disrespectful.

Surrounding yourself with yes people is the biggest mistake any leader can make. It sucks the creativity out of the organization and can lead to disastrous outcomes as we all have read in one of our classics, *The Emperor's New Clothes* by Hans Christian Andersen!

At *Shark Tank India*, the beauty of the platform was that it put five Sharks, five Type-A personalities, all with strong views and strong voices in one room. As expected, this resulted in debates and the best outcome for the founders and the show. How, you might ask.

Well, there were two forms of dissent at *Shark Tank India*:

Sharks' Dissent with the Founders

The obvious one was with the founder where Sharks obviously disagreed on various issues, with the most common and pertinent one being valuation. There were also disagreements on branding, packaging, pricing, and scalability. The other common disagreement was always on the founders spreading themselves too thin with too many SKUs and the Sharks wanting to see focus on fewer products. This feedback was invaluable for those who got funded and even those who didn't. Most Sharks have created large businesses, and their learnings from their successes and failures were shared through such dissent and discussion.

Sharks' Dissent among Themselves

However, the most interesting dissent was when Sharks disagreed with one another.

We all come from different industries, different schools of thought and strong opinions are bound to be expressed.

I remember all of us having debates on other larger topics too. For example, husband–wife teams as co-founders and how some investors consciously didn't prefer this while others did. I also remember us having varying opinions on the same founder. There were strong founders who counter argued and challenged us—this trait was welcomed by some as having courage of conviction. Others felt that it showed that they weren't open to feedback and not easy to work with. I had strong debates on women-centric issues where I disagreed with certain comments made by the male Sharks, especially in the case of Good Good Piggy and Hemp India pitches. We also disagreed on whether mentors added value or not. Then there were very specific pitches that come to mind. I will narrate some here to demonstrate the type of issues we disagreed on. Again, is there a right answer? The jury is out and only time will tell ... but it's always interesting to hear two views and opinions on the same issue!

I remember debating with Anupam on the name of a venture, Scrapshaala. This was a mother- daughter duo that made art items out of scrap. Anupam felt that the name might have a negative connotation whereas I felt that the word scrap in the name was an asset as it showed that this was a purpose-driven brand built around sustainability. Another dissent I had with Anupam was on the market size and scalability of Insurance Samadhan, a venture that helps customers with solving issues around pending insurance claims. He felt the market for it was small whereas I felt that as insurance penetration in our country grows, the market size could become pretty large. The reason I didn't invest in them is due to gaps around their working capital cycle.

They had to wait for long for payments from consumers after solving their problems and this resulted in their cash getting blocked, bringing up the risk of bad debts. This could be a serious drain on profitability and cash flow as they scaled. When a founder wanted Aman for his brand building expertise, Ashneer disagreed on many occasions saying that founders should focus on getting the right valuation and not just a single-minded skill that a particular investor is strong at. Ashneer wanted Menstrupedia to be a sanitary pad company; I wanted them to focus on content creation and education. Peyush wanted Altor, the smart helmet start-up to focus on technology and accident emergency services whereas Aman and I also wanted them to focus on the helmet/product angle. Namhya tea, the product around Ayurveda claimed to solve several health issues. Vineeta wasn't sold on the merits of Ayurveda, particularly on their pitch around solving issues around menstruation. However, Aman saw value in it and invested in that venture.

During the Otua EV three-wheeler pitch, I had a debate over legacy companies vs new age companies in the EV world, what strengths one brought vs the other, and who would dominate in the long run. My co-Sharks were betting on new age companies as they believed that these companies could pivot and innovate faster. I disagreed for a few reasons—while it is true that many legacy companies refuse to see the writing on the wall (Nokia, Kodak), there are ample examples of legacy companies which demonstrate speed, scale and disruption to reinvent themselves. On the show, I gave the example of Pune-based Bajaj Auto that has constantly innovated to become the most valuable two-wheeler company globally. Rajiv Bajaj has often been quoted as saying that 'only the paranoid survive . . .' I am betting that the legacy companies will continue to stay paranoid and not complacent and will go on to become dominant players in the EV space through innovation and the power of strong balance sheets. Regardless, it was interesting to hear these diverse views from Sharks on the emerging EV landscape.

Very often, when the arguments got heated with dissenting views, one of the Sharks would intervene and help cool things off. Each one did this in their own unique styles. Aman would crack a joke and use his boyish charm to make the moment lighter. Anupam would put on his seasoned investor hat, calmly summarize the key discussion points and ask the rest to stay focused. I played the role of the annoying school monitor who would often jump in to remind everyone that enough time had been spent on debates and that it was time to make a decision.

Shark Tank India was a masterclass for Indian households in the nuances of the business world, how different leaders think, what key focus areas are and how these leaders have different perspectives. Along with management terms, *Shark Tank India* highlighted the value of dissent and the richness it brings to any discussion and decision-making process.

Cultivating Dissent in an Organization

In my opinion, the following four changes have helped us foster dissent at Emcure.

First and foremost, right hiring is important. Look for people who will use the power of their voice and have the courage and conviction to speak up. Certain smartly placed questions in the course of interviews easily highlight the presence or absence of this important trait. Qualities that ensure dissent are curiosity and courage. So, in our interviews for potential hires at Emcure, we always ask a question: Tell me when your curiosity has helped you challenge and change the status quo? Another question we ask is: Tell me when you have spoken up and disagreed openly and what was the result of that?

Secondly, another policy to be put in place is to reward and celebrate dissent through promotions, public praise in meetings and awards. In several meetings, when people disagree with me, I am open to changing my point of view if I am convinced of the logic, even if it's contrary to my earlier position. I make it a point to praise the opposing view in that meeting as well as cite that example in my other corporate talks. In addition, I also regularly conduct town hall meetings where the team is encouraged to ask any question and a no-holds-barred discussion typically takes place. This sends a signal down the line that dissent is welcome. As leaders, we need to walk the talk.

Thirdly, departments typically work in silos and it becomes incumbent upon the management to create projects that require cross-functional teams to meet, debate and discuss with each other. One example that is fairly common in most companies is that R&D and marketing rarely meet. They work in silos resulting in ad hoc product launches. Both departments then blame each other when new products fail. We started having regular meetings between all stakeholders and this has ensured that the identification of molecules, product development and launches are more well-thought-out after taking into consideration diverse views.

Fourth, and the most important aspect to be kept in mind for dissent to achieve its desired outcome—it must always be on the basis of unshakeable facts and not merely a judgement call. Very often, due to personal biases, ego clashes, people dissent to take jabs at each other and this is where a strong facilitator is needed. Someone who keeps the discussion objective and fact-based and does not let these egos come in the way is critical so that dissent is not a weapon for personal agendas but rather an important tool for organizational success.

Finally, good founders listen to this dissent, appreciate constructive feedback and contrary views, mull over it but always combine their analytical thinking, dissent and instinct to make the decision that is in the best interest of the organization.

Chapter 9

The Power of Networks

The Renal Project is a venture that provides affordable dialysis options in tier-2 cities and interiors, a venture I wanted to invest in at any cost. Ashneer offered a better valuation but I won the deal because Aman and I were able to convince the founder about the power of my networks. I explained to the founder, Shashank, how my company Emcure's network of nephrologists and hospitals could truly take his venture to the next level and that powerful statement clinched the deal for us.

We spend so much of our time and energy planning our degrees and our work experience, but barely spend any methodical thinking, planning and time to develop our networks.

Networks have helped me in both my personal and professional growth. If you want to be a lifelong learner, surrounding yourself with the right set of personal and professional folks helps—they inspire you, teach you, challenge you and truly help you grow.

Benefits of Good Networks

Networks are an important strength that good investors bring to an entrepreneur—a network of HNIs and investors for the next fundraise, network of business leaders from companies that can be strategic partners for the entrepreneur, network of distribution channels that can help them scale in India and globally.

Most co-founder teams at *Shark Tank India* (other than family members) were either college friends or work colleagues. You find the right people with the same purpose, passion, complimentary skills and you hit gold. Having co-founders can exponentially strengthen the leadership bandwidth and the ability to divide and conquer.

Networks help you get customer referrals, word-of-mouth marketing and provide crucial testimonials. Even those doing jobs need networks both within and outside the organization. Networks within, especially sponsors, act as mentors and champion your career growth. Networks outside are critical too. For example, according to a report by LinkedIn, 85 per cent job vacancies are filled through networking!

Developing the Right Networks

There are a few tips I have learned along the way to help with networking.

- Research and join relevant associations and be part of the right peer group. Entrepreneurs have limited time given the multiple priorities on their schedule on any given day. Every hour spent at a conference has an 'opportunity cost' of that hour that could have been spent on building your business. So choose your networking events wisely.

- Research on the attendees and pick the 2–3 that you will walk up to and make a sincere connect with. Building that emotional connect is important. Remember, quality over quantity, always.

- Practice the art of introducing yourself effectively. The ability to walk in, have the courage to introduce yourself, hand your business card and ask the right questions is important. A good tip is to keep a few interesting ice-breaker questions and topics handy.

- Really listen. When you make this effort, you understand what is important to the other person. This can help you quickly deduce how you can best add value to the relationship and make the other person want to stay connected with you as well. Also, by listening, you are giving someone the opportunity to do what they like to do the most—talk about themselves!

- After the event, it is important to follow up shortly, say in 12–24 hours, with a crisp and action-oriented email.

- I also make it a point to keep records of people I have met, those who I want to stay connected with, what I liked about them, interesting stories, what makes them click, etc. It may seem small but it's often these little things that make the big difference.

To network, you also need the ability to cold call and keep at it till one out of every twenty emails and calls gets you the desired response. This is not a task for the faint-hearted or ones with fragile egos. You have to have the resilience to accept 99 per cent 'nos' for that one 'yes' that you want to hear. When I started my entrepreneurs' academy, I did not know anyone from the start-up world, neither entrepreneurs nor investors. I managed to Google their emails and wrote to so many. Few actually made the effort to reply and these relationships are ones I treasure till date.

Another effective method is to use your existing contacts to refer you to networks that will help you. Tapping into the alumni network of your college is another great way. Once you learn this art, you will be amazed at how you can chat up even random people at a gym, community event or school event to make connections and use them towards the right goals. It's an art and it takes practice.

Once you establish contact with the right network, building an emotional connect is the most important thing to do, so that this can be a relationship with depth and longevity to get desired outcomes. At business school, many of my classmates took up golf since golf clubs continue to be one of the most common networking spaces in the US. Over offsites and weekends, employees bond over golf. Sport is an obsession and reading up and staying up to date on various sports and teams was a tough weekend task for an ignorant person like me. But it is essential in order to be a smart contributor at work lunches and dinners where more often than not, conversations veer around sports. Find out what makes your network tick, what gets them excited and read up on it so that you can bond and develop a personal rapport around that.

Another important aspect is the ability to ask for things and not be worried about rejection and failure. At most, people will say no, but that's okay. Unless you have specific asks of your networks, it will not help you. I had a very tough time asking for things, due to shyness, fear of hearing 'no' and awkwardness. Many emotions would run through my head but that's where self-training helps. Push yourself to do tough things enough and it becomes a habit over a period of time. The awkwardness gets replaced with ease and comfort so the key is to be at it and keep doing it.

If you are an introvert, you may be a bit intimidated by the concept of networking. The only way is to keep pushing yourself to go to more such events and speak up. Initially, take along a friend who understands you, pushes you and provides that much-needed mental support. Use your networks to network, which means that you must ask your friends and colleagues to make the introductions, either personally or through email. Introverts prefer one-on-one conversations so try to catch the person you want to speak to, either by showing up early or finding them alone, say while they are walking down the hallway or grabbing a cup of coffee.

But one word of caution. Whether you are an extrovert or introvert, networking must be scheduled and you should learn to be selective. It can be a real energy- and time-guzzler if you don't manage this smartly and feel the need to go to each and every event that comes up due to typical FOMO (fear of missing out) which can be counterproductive.

Networking is always with a definite purpose so only go to those events that fit with a well thought-out plan.

Also remember that there is a difference between networking and socializing. Networking is done with a very clear objective of adding value to your business or personal growth. It is done in a very structured manner. Socializing is lighter and for relaxing.

In fact, I wanted to share a personal story of how *Shark Tank India* was pure destiny and a result of networks. I am a member of Tie Mumbai and one of our board members is Apoorva Ranjan Sharma, the founder of Venture Catalysts, a fund involved with *Shark Tank India*. I approached him to request that one of the teens from my entrepreneurship academy be given the opportunity to pitch on the show as this is fairly common on *Shark Tank India* USA. The very next day, his team called me back and asked me if I would like to be a Shark! One thing led to another and this golden opportunity came by as a result of tapping into one of my networks.

Stories shaped me, and made me dream big. I wanted to write a book with stories that would inspire others to do the same! I had started this journey with a good and noble intent in my heart. However, while writing this book, my initial experience was a very negative one. I had sent two chapters to a publisher who did not like them. The publisher didn't even get on a call or meet me to share feedback. They just sent me a few WhatsApp messages saying that the chapters weren't honest and real at all. I felt very demotivated as a first-time writer who had poured her heart out. I disagreed with the publisher. I felt there was a lot of honesty in the book as I had written about many uncomfortable topics, setbacks, and deeply personal episodes. Also, in the interest of keeping it raw and authentic, I had made the effort to write every single word myself vs getting some reputed writer to pen it down for me. Regardless, even with all my inherent positivity and self-confidence, I was ready to give up. That's when my inner voice asked me to connect with Harsh Mariwala, chairman of Marico Ltd, to get a second opinion. I had read his biography and loved it. I still have his voice message where he told me not to get discouraged and give it one more shot. He introduced me to a lovely young girl, Radhika Marwah from Penguin, and we instantly bonded. Besides supporting the project, she made some great suggestions which improved the readability and flow of the book. This is another example of a strong network coming through for me and helping me see through the clutter of my own mind. Today, I am doing something I have always wanted to do—write a book full of honest and inspiring stories to push others to dream big. I will always be grateful to Mr Mariwala for encouraging and supporting me.

An entrepreneur's journey is a long and lonely one. Networks act as co-founders, as friends, mentors, investors, and support groups that can help you scale and be partners and collaborators in this journey. Seek these networks, invest time and energy, nurture these networks and then watch their power lift your personal and professional growth to an entirely new level!

Chapter 10

Family Business Dynamics

Family businesses make up for an astonishing 79 per cent of India's GDP. I was thrilled to see many ventures started by family members at *Shark Tank India*. There were parent–son/ daughter teams; siblings and couples as co-founders! That got me thinking about the unique nuances of a family business.

Advantages of a Family Business

Let's look at the lifecycle of a typical new venture. When starting up, family members are the natural choice as co-founders for many reasons.

Firstly, there is an innate emotional connect and trust among family members that brings in the passion and energy that all start-ups need. I remember Morikko Pure Foods at *Shark Tank India* and how the son and daughter spoke with so much pride about their father, about how he had overcome many hardships and the awe they felt about the way he fasted and his energy levels. I can tell from my own experience that it's a privilege to learn from the best, who, in my case too, is my father.

Secondly, a family business can tap into the experience and knowledge of the older generation. For example, in Beyond Water, the brother-sister duo had got their degree from one of the best colleges, Babson University in USA. But they had their uncle involved in the venture as he had run their tea business for years and had the manufacturing and distribution expertise to guide and help them.

Thirdly, there is an easier definition of roles and designations when family is involved. This is typically based on age and/or family hierarchy which makes matters simpler to define and follow.

Pitfalls of a Family Business

However, as the business scales, there are many pitfalls associated with family business dynamics that founders need to be cognizant of and take the right measures at the right time.

Firstly, the real risk of what happens if things go sour and don't work out. This is especially critical for couples that work together. Working together when all is well can be a value-add but if things don't work out, it can have permanent and irreparable damage on the marriage and children.

Secondly, very often, the presence of too many family members prevents professionals from joining the company which can be to the detriment of the overall growth and culture of the organization. Investors are also wary of investing in such businesses due to the fear of such rifts and also concerns on whether the best professional talent would want to join. A related point is that employees should feel comfortable while disagreeing with family members. Developing this culture and work ethic, if you have family members with a lot of ego in the mix, isn't always an easy task.

Thirdly, board composition and overall corporate governance is not taken as seriously. Getting a good number of independent experts on the board is crucial not just for optics but due to the fact that it often brings fresh and diverse perspectives to any strategic discussion taken up at a board level. Having established and reputed internal and external auditors and consultants also shows willingness and openness to feedback.

Finally, succession planning is always an area that is never clearly addressed in most family businesses. The founder, at times, develops a God-like personality and doesn't want to retire at the right age. This makes the next generation restless. Lack of clear succession planning impacts the business for sure. However, the next generation also needs to demonstrate, through their work ethic, discipline and persistence, that they have succeeded in projects given to them and are, therefore, ready and deserving to take on this higher responsibility.

Ways to Solve for the Pitfalls of a Family Business

Needless to say, the above areas must be addressed.

Firstly, ensure that family members get the right credentials in the form of education and work experience prior to joining the business and the roles they are given are a good fit for their interest, education and experience. It must be clarified whether they will be expected to work ground up or start in an executive role when they join the business. Everything must be discussed and aligned ahead of time to avoid heartburn. Annual structured appraisals for family members, facilitated by an external business coach or a trusted board member, are absolutely essential to discuss what is going well and what needs improvement.

Secondly, there should be a good mix of professionals at the senior-most decision-making levels with complete autonomy to do what they want and disagree with family members when and where they deem right. Similarly, family members must also be empowered so that they don't feel stifled by 'old-timers' who often resist change. If they don't have the freedom to bring in younger leaders, new systems and new ideas, they will not feel the sense of ownership that is the strength of a family business.

Thirdly, there must be a good set of guides and arbitrators. This is key to ensuring success. In our business, there are two wings of the family involved and choosing a person that both trust is important. This could, at times, be a board member, a family friend or even a family member who is not connected with the business in any way. When there is a deadlock, a trustworthy arbitrator's role is absolutely priceless.

Given the high percentage of family businesses in India, most entrepreneurs need to be crystal clear about what the potential issues could be when they start a business as a family. What are the demerits (such as the ones listed above) and have they thought through ways to deal with them? Can they be clearer about discussing, and getting closure on succession plans and put them down in writing rather than leaving the second generation guessing? If the second generation is not interested, are they able to get a professional CEO to run the organization? Can they put in systems and a culture that attracts the most talented professionals to join them? Are they wise and generous enough to offer equity for retaining these professionals?

My Experience of Working in a Family Business

My personal experience of working in a family business has been mixed. I have been privileged to watch and learn from my visionary father, enjoyed scaling the business, building big brands and creating value for all stakeholders, it has also been a tough journey in many ways. What helped me the most in my journey is my strong education background and six-plus years of work experience in the US. I would strongly urge the next generation to get external work experience before joining their family business.

In spite of this, I did face many road blocks put in place by insecure old-timers when I wanted to bring in new systems and usher in digitization. Let me share an instance of how I faced resistance and what I did to resolve it in the interest of the organization. I am a strong believer in the role of data analytics and sales force automation in marketing as I had done it first-hand while at Guidant. When I presented this to the senior management at Emcure, I was mocked and these systems were dismissed. Rather than giving up, I went on to hire my own sales force effectiveness and data analytics teams in a separate location. (I was CFO at the time and worked out of a different location than my father and the marketing teams). Medical reps were filling in data related to doctor visits anyway but there was no one using this data for strategic decision-making.

A lot of insights from this data were very valuable. For example, areas that had low sales and low doctor visits meant that those reps needed to be pushed to meet doctor coverage norms and their KRAs had to be adjusted to ensure this got implemented. Areas that had low sales and high doctor visits meant those reps were struggling and needed training and field work assistance from seniors. Areas where the reps were too high or too low in count needed adjustments. Also, data analytics identified areas where one division selling products for pregnancy was doing exceptionally well and the other division selling other molecules for pregnancy was struggling. The solution was to ensure that the doctors who were believers in the products doing well had to be leveraged to cross-sell products of the struggling divison. These were quick wins that only data can enable. Small changes like these could have a huge impact on sales as I had seen in my job at Guidant. After days of persistence and showing these reports and their impact, my father was convinced and marketing teams too started presenting this data in their monthly MIS to the CEO. A battle had been won and credibility established through higher sales.

Many such instances later, I felt that the time had come to ask for what I wanted—to be given a chance to lead India sales. However, I was called a 'finance' person who would not be able to do it. I had to seek the help of two board members who believed in me to convince my father to take a chance. Once I took over this portfolio, I tried my very best to take everyone along. But somewhere along the way, I reluctantly reached the conclusion that a few old-timers would not adapt to my ways and replacing them was essential. These gentlemen had contributed tremendously in the past but did not belong to the future. They were not willing to change and be open to what was required for the next stage of scaling up the company. It wasn't easy. It was painful but required. After months of presenting evidence of how important new initiatives were being blocked, I was permitted to do this.

I essentially brought four big changes in the India business:

1) data analytics and digitization
2) younger leadership
3) cost optimization initiatives to grow EBITDA and
4) focus on making big brands bigger

But the journey wasn't easy. There would be micro management from my father. At times, he would openly overrule my decisions in public which created its own sets of issues. All these had to be handled with firmness, at times, and at other times, with a sensitive emotional touch.

Pharma is a traditional industry and I knew that infusion of fresh ideas would only help make it better. Becoming an angel investor or launching my entrepreneurship academy was my way of challenging myself, learning from new age companies, and adopting new styles of marketing. However, my decision to do both of these was met with resistance. My father saw these as distractions from my role at Emcure. It took me time to convince him that these side ventures would actually help me meet new people, bring in fresh perspectives which eventually would make me a stronger leader at Emcure! There is no secret formula to handling this type of resistance. You have to keep trying new techniques. Some work, some don't, but you stay at it.

As mentioned before, clarity of roles is most important in family businesses. In my family, my husband, Vik, is in charge of Corporate Strategy and Finance including Mergers and Acquisitions as well as all capital raising initiatives. He is also vice chairman and board member of our US business. My brother Samit oversees R&D, manufacturing and our biotech subsidiary. Most importantly, he plays a critical role in portfolio selection. Two of our cousins are part of the business as well. One of them is an executive board member and is responsible for capital expenditure projects. The other manages commercial operations for the group in addition to overseeing the emerging markets business vertical. So, we all have clearly defined roles and don't get in each other's way. This helps in the balancing act of building the business while, at the same time, keeping the family together.

Though I have had my share of good and bad experiences, I can truly say that overall, it's a blessing and a privilege to be a second-generation business owner. I never take it for granted. I always look at it with humility and gratitude.

My biggest advice for the next generation is that be prepared for these challenges, stay patient and persistent. My advice for the founder would be to try to ensure that these issues are proactively addressed so that the beautiful venture that they have created not only outlasts them but also becomes stronger and better in the future. Family dynamics, if not handled well, can be energy- and time-guzzlers and therefore, this education and sharing of best practices must be a prerequisite for anyone setting out on this wonderful yet double-edged journey!

Here are excerpts from an interview I did with siblings Devang and Shachi of Beyond Water (premium water enhancer) from *Shark Tank India* that demonstrates some dynamics and learnings of family businesses.

Their family is in the tea business while the siblings have branched out into a more new-age beverage business. To me, the biggest lesson from their story is that it is a fabulous thing when the next generation uses the family business to start something related that is their own. It gives them freedom and a distinct identity but, at the same time, keeps the founder of the family business involved and engaged in the new venture.

Namita: Devang and Shachi, when and why did you decide to quit the family business and start your own venture?

Devang & Shachi: Our family is in the tea business and after our graduation from Babson University, USA, we started off as contract manufacturers in the tea business. We were not excited by this business, as we found the industry very traditional. We wanted to start something where we could cater to the younger generation and bring in innovation. We felt that as individuals and entrepreneurs, we would grow a lot more in this new venture.

Namita: What were some of the benefits of the family business and family members?

Devang & Shachi: My uncle is our sounding board and so is my mother, who has been in the family business for the past twenty-five years. Due to their breadth of experience, they are able to guide us. This is a huge asset for us. Additionally, when we started our business, unlike other start-ups, we did not have to struggle for seed capital, as our family and friends supported us. This helped us focus on the business rather than fundraising. Basics like financials, legal compliances, and registrations were also easier as we had experts and consultants from our family business to guide us through all this. Most important were the networks that our family business brought us—folks with FMCG businesses, credible manufacturers, and R&D experts who helped us with the formulation, etc.

Namita: How is it working with a sibling? All siblings fight growing up but how do you handle your differences while growing your business?

Devang & Shachi: We both have complementary skills. We recognize each other's strengths and whenever there is a deadlock, we typically decide that the person with the strength in that area will take the final decision. We are both invested in this venture and it's the passion to see it succeed that helps us figure out ways to get things done!

Chapter 11

Women Breaking Barriers

In a country where the female workforce participation has gone from 27 per cent to as low as 19 per cent[*] during the pandemic, what irks me more than this shocking statistic is all of us being in denial mode. What I mean is that several men, and often women too, are clueless about the biases that women in our country are subject to and think that it is indeed a thing of the past. When a country has such dismal statistics, we need more women to speak up, have their voices heard, their opinions and their struggles highlighted. Most importantly, we need a non-judgemental society that doesn't instantly label this as 'self-victimizing feminist behaviour'. Well, if it were really a thing of the past, we would not have such tragic

---

[*] Labor Force Participation Rate, Female (Percentage of Female Population Ages Fifteen-Plus) (Modeled ILO Estimate) – India', https://data.worldbank.org/indicator/SL.TLF.CACT.FE.ZS?locations=IN

workforce participation numbers nor would we have global numbers such as this: only 2.3 per cent[**] of women-led ventures got funded in 2020! So can we get out of denial mode and into action mode?

Do women still get judged? Sometimes directly or sometimes in hushed tones for any or all of the following?

- Will she come back after her maternity leave or get too attached to the baby?
- Will she relocate if her husband does?
- Will she be able to put in the long hours and travel the job demands?
- Will she be able to handle harsh feedback?

All of the above and more are harsh realities even today and not a thing of the past!

Well, the good thing about *Shark Tank India* is that many of these issues were addressed head-on and the show gave a platform for strong, feisty women entrepreneurs to showcase their talent, their drive, their resilience and get funded!

I loved interacting with the following women on the show:

- Rakhi Pal of Eventbeep unapologetically shared that she was ok with her family disowning her but she would not give up on her dreams.
- Aishwarya Biswas of skincare brand Auli refused to accept feedback that she needed a co-founder and could not go solo. Of course she could go solo, was her comeback.
- Jayanti Bhattacharya of India Hemp and Company

[**] Women-Led Startups Received Just 2.3% of VC Funding in 2020. https://hbr.org/2021/02/women-led-startups-received-just-2-3-of-vc-funding-in-2020

got upset when she was told that it seemed that her venture was a hobby for her. She asked point-blank if this 'hobby' remark was being made because she was a woman! If Sharks can be blunt and ask tough questions, why can't she? After all, it's her equity that she is taking a call on.

- Aditi Gupta of Menstrupedia talked about how she would break taboos around periods, no matter what it took.

- Purva Aggarwal of Good Good Piggy did not shed a tear and kept smiling even after thirty minutes of the harshest feedback I have personally witnessed in a long time!

- Rubal Chib of QZense took massive offence to being told she was wasting the Sharks' time. She spoke up in clear terms of how her pregnant co-founder Srishti Batra would not have driven from Bangalore in the eighth month of her pregnancy, if they didn't believe in their venture. She agreed that the valuation asked for was unrealistic but they were not here to waste our time, she repeated firmly.

And it wasn't just limited to these women speaking up. There were so many others who broke stereotypes in their own unique style. My favourite ones were the sisters-in-law from Darbhanga making Jhaji pickles. The way those women rattled off MBA buzzwords would put even seasoned investors to shame! Sanskriti Dawle, the CEO of Thinkerbell, was incredible, and the way she stood her ground and negotiated with five fierce Sharks and got her desired valuation was pure joy to watch! At *Shark Tank India*, 49 per cent of ventures that got funded had women co-founders . . . just wow!

Not just the three women Sharks but all the male Sharks too sincerely considered funding ventures with female founders that showed potential and that was brilliant!

As a working woman, I have faced struggles of my own. There are times I have asked questions in meetings and the men have looked at my father while answering them. It was amusing to see Indra Nooyi talk about similar experiences in her autobiography. When I got pregnant, there were murmurs about whether I would return to work and if they would need an interim CFO. When I did come back to work and asked for a flexible schedule in the first year, I was labelled 'part-time' by many. The reality of senior women committed to their jobs is that regardless of time spent in the office, you are always working and never part time!

There are some real issues that working women face and I would like to touch upon a few here.

The Parenting Trap

Women, these days, choose to delay children or not have children due to careers. This is entirely their decision and needs to be respected and not judged. (Just consider freezing your eggs in case you change your mind). If there are infertility issues and the couple opt for IVF, the woman needs flexible work options as this is one of the most physically, financially and emotionally trying times. The couple need all the possible support they can get. Once they have had kids, they need a strong flex work policy at the workplace and affordable and safe childcare so that they can focus on their work. Indra Nooyi has spoken at length about the urgent need for accessible and affordable childcare in her book. This is grossly missing in developed and developing countries and largely handicaps women from returning to the workforce.

My parenting journey hasn't been easy either. I had a wonderful mother who was always there when I couldn't make it to doctor appointments or parent-teacher meetings. But the labels continue even today. At times, I have been labelled as an absentee mother and selfish when I have prioritized my dreams and aspirations. If my son got a lower score in school or his fever persisted longer than average, I was held responsible for not being physically present enough to manage. It hurts to hear all this but you have to remember that it's always a balancing act. Sometimes, you make children your priority. But, at times when you can't, don't beat yourself up. Stay indifferent. Don't let these comments impact you; just keep on balancing and juggling the best you can. You will never be the perfect mom and that's ok, as long as your conscience says that you have tried your best.

Being Financially Independent

Another common trap that educated working women fall into is completely delegating their personal finances to their spouses. They have no clue about the amount of their savings, where it is invested and annual returns. It is extremely important for women to take charge of their personal finances and be educated on the details so that they have **contingency planning** in place. It is fairly simple and doesn't take too long. Then why won't we make the effort?

When a woman has an entrepreneur husband, she needs to communicate clearly on financial matters. It is possible that she may be a working professional and a steady income earner or a homemaker while he is pursuing his entrepreneurial dream. It is very important to discuss financial plans with your husband. It is easy for entrepreneurs to get so caught up in their ambitions that they underestimate the impact it will have on their partner. If he is taking a big loan, how does he intend to pay it back, what is the security/mortgage, are you comfortable with it, etc., are questions that need to be asked. Overall, what is the extent of financial risk that he is signing up for, what is the contingency plan if the venture doesn't work and what is the extent of savings that will not be touched no matter what—these are discussions that have to be had and both need to be clear and on the same page. This same discussion is required if the woman chooses to be the entrepreneur.

Fitness

Here, I would like to talk about the importance of mental and physical fitness. Like everything else, this becomes low priority or is usually pursued as the occasional do-or-die diet for an upcoming wedding or event. Unless this becomes a consistent activity, and an integral part of our lives, we will not get the benefits of high productivity that will help us reach our full potential.

As a teen and young adult, I went through massive emotional eating due to stress. As a result, before my tenth and twelfth class boards, when I was alone in the US for the first time, and during other such occasions, I would put on almost 20–25 pounds, feel crappy about myself and then go on crazy diets to lose weight. Over the last ten years, I have become super disciplined about my physical fitness.

I work out six days a week and do a combination of functional training, yoga, dance aerobics and evening walks. I stopped dieting as I saw it impacting my skin and made me look dehydrated and dull. For me, a few extra pounds are ok, but your face must radiate a healthy glow even without make-up. I have achieved this with a gluten-free diet and ensuring that I eat and sleep early on most days. Being a vegetarian and a teetotaller have helped. I believe in the power of Ayurveda and homeopathy to build a strong immune system. Eating soaked almonds first thing in the morning, having a cooling drink in summer, the power of turmeric, and such other small things in your daily routine can really rejuvenate you. What I started really late is meditation. It is a must to detach and stay calm and positive. Given the number of changes a woman's body and health go through right from periods to pregnancy to mid-age hormonal issues, it is critical to stay fit as this helps in maintaining work productivity. However, women don't prioritize their health, don't prioritize their fitness and don't realize that investing in physical and mental fitness is as important as investing in good books or a good seminar to keep yourself productive and sharp!

Feedback

At Emcure and other places, I have often seen women limiting themselves. They stop themselves from asking for that much-deserved raise or promotion during appraisals. They don't promote themselves and their work enough. Change this. Speak up more often. I have also seen many get defensive or emotional when objective and harsh yet well-meaning feedback is given. When you react strongly, it puts your manager on guard and you will lose out on the growth and fulfillment that comes from being a patient and open listener. However, you may not always agree with the feedback given and this must be politely yet firmly put across. Let me share my personal experience on this. I have been told several times during my appraisal that I speak too loudly and that I need to speak softer; I speak too much and I am too direct. I did not agree with this as I felt that my unique personality (talking and joking) is what helps me break the ice and build bonds with my team and external stakeholders. This trait is unique to me and something I am proud of. As long as I am getting the desired outcomes, I don't feel the need to change.

Be the Change You Want to See

Firstly, we need to stop being in denial and accept that these statistics need to change. Second, we need to stop labelling and judging as a society. Third and most importantly, we need to have a more accepting support system for women. On average, Indian women perform six hours of unpaid housework a day v/s the average Indian man who puts in an hour a day. Can we have more men help out, more family support and better childcare? Lastly, women need to be proud of the power of their voices. They need to speak up more and have more women role models who empower them to do all of the above. Kiran Shaw is one woman role model who I am close to and personally admire. She uses the power of her voice to support the right causes. While I was talking to a dear friend, Zia Mody, one of India's most reputed lawyers and business leaders, we discussed how a couple of small steps can go a long way in ensuring we have more women at the workplace. Firstly, for every role, have your HR send you at least two resumes of women for every five that are sent in for that vacancy. Secondly, diversity goals should be built into KRAs of senior leaders. These direct policies and signals are important if we want to change the statistics.

So let's all pledge to change these statistics and mindsets. This, indeed, is the beauty of the entertainment world and shows like *Shark Tank India* and I am so proud to be part of a show that truly showcased stories of courage and candour by women founders that touched our hearts and hopefully busted stereotypes and changed many mindsets along the way!

My Five Key Lessons for Women:

1) **Get rid of the guilt:** I often say that women are great at time management but terrible at guilt management. I feel it's a mental disorder that we need to work on. A simple example: When I miss my child's school event for a work commitment, I feel guilty. If I were to be a homemaker, I would have felt guilty about wasting my degrees. There is no right answer. Each to her own. Whatever your decision and your path, make peace with it and stop beating yourself up!

2) **It's okay to be labelled selfish**: Women feel bad when they make time for themselves, their needs, and their dreams. It is important to take this time to refresh and rejuvenate one's body and soul. If you take care of yourself and are happy, you will be a better mother, wife, daughter, employer and employee!

3) **Ask for help and not permission**: Women don't ask for help. They wonder what 'people might think' or 'they may find me incompetent, etc.' But that's not the case. Everyone should ask for help whenever needed. You will be surprised how many well-meaning family members, friends and colleagues are happy to chip in. You don't need to be a perfectionist or superwoman.

4) **Learn to listen to your inner voice**: Trust your gut instinct. Take time to be in touch with your intuition and like Steve Jobs said, 'Don't let the voice of others drown your inner voice.' This also means that once we learn to trust our inner voice as our biggest teacher, we must learn to ignore labels and stop seeking external validation.

5) **Don't limit yourself**: Women have a habit of blaming others, especially society. We create our own mental barriers and stop ourselves from reaching our true potential. Stop doing that. Dare to dream really big dreams.

In summary, take pride in being flawsome (awesome in spite of your flaws) and always remember my favourite line, 'Be you. The world will adjust!'

Interviews with Women Entrepreneurs Sanskriti Dhawale, Aditi Gupta and Aishwarya Biswas from *Shark Tank India*

Sanskriti Dhawale of Thinkerbell, a Device That Teaches Braille to the Visually Impaired

Namita: How did you think of this venture? Where did the idea come from?

Sanskriti: While studying engineering at BITS, I participated in a hackathon with a few friends and worked on a project that was around teaching Braille. At that point, we had worked on this purely from a tech solution angle. We visited schools for the blind to get more insights and that's when we saw two things. Firstly, thirteen- and fourteen-year-olds are not literate in even something as basic as the letters of the alphabet in Braille. This prompted us to learn Braille and we realized that in spite of being engineers, it was a very difficult language even for us to master. Secondly, teachers were amazed by this technology and wanted to place orders for their schools. We realized there was a gap and there could be a business opportunity around this. We all had a passion for social impact and had worked for various NGOs. Once we sensed the need for this, we were excited to get started.

Namita: How did you manage to get your first round of believers and funding?

Sanskriti: By this time, we were participating in all sorts of Business Plan competitions. In our final year, we participated in one by the UK Department of International Trade. We won the competition and were invited to a demo for the royal family visiting India. This is where Mr Anand Mahindra and Mr Saurabh Srivastav from Indian Angel Network heard our pitch and invested in us. This was followed by a round by Let's Venture.

Namita: How has life changed after *Shark Tank India*?

Sanskriti: People believe in us and many are approaching us to learn more about the product. Our product always had challenges getting through airport security due to the Braille stylist in our device but the high point was a recent trip where the security not just recognized us and cleared us quickly but also had the most endearing ten-minute conversation on Prathamesh!

Namita: There are very few women in tech and even fewer entrepreneurs who get funding. What inspired you to get into engineering and entrepreneurship?

Sanskriti: My mother is my biggest inspiration. She completed her engineering, went on to study architecture, LLB and more recently got a PhD at the age of fifty-seven. She never stops pushing herself.

She founded an architecture consulting firm and is a passionate entrepreneur. When you have such a role model at home, its pushes you to dream big!

Aditi Gupta of Menstrupedia, a Venture That Educates and Breaks Taboos around Periods

Namita: Aditi, how has the journey been in terms of busting taboos around a topic like periods? Was it tough initially and then did it get easier?

Aditi: Honestly, we have had a very positive experience. When we took this up, we got a lot of support and encouragement from all quarters. We never faced any setbacks other than one incident where an FIR was filed against us for a poster that someone found offensive. The one bottleneck was finding investors who believed this idea could scale.

Investors were often older men who didn't even know how their own daughters were educated about periods. They asked amusing questions like how will this pay for your bills; they doubted the revenue model and needless to say, we didn't get any funding. What helped us was the crowdfunding platform where we collected Rs 5 lakh very effortlessly and this was enough to get us started on our mission.

Namita: How has it been being a woman co-founder? Did you experience any biases?

Aditi: Quite the contrary! In fact, being a woman in this space, I am able to explain periods better and answer questions with a lot more ease and expertise. I always speak from my heart. I believe in unfiltered emotions when giving my training sessions and this has been much appreciated. In fact, I have received several awards and recognitions for this from several institutions that specifically celebrate women entrepreneurs. The only interesting fact is that when my husband Tuhin started speaking on this issue, people were not comfortable and wanted me to speak instead of him. So being a man was a weakness and being a woman worked in my favour.

Aishwarya Biswas of Auli, a Premium Ayurveda Skincare Brand

Namita: Aishwarya, you started your pitch with 'Main apni favourite hoon' (I am my favourite person). I just loved that but I know there were other Sharks who misunderstood this to mean self-obsessed and possibly tough to work with. Do you hear these contrary views often?

Aishwarya: All the time! I spent thirty-five years of my life prioritizing everyone but myself. At thirty-five, I had a eureka moment and swore to prioritize myself and follow my dreams. I am proud of this and have no regrets. I am who I am. Anyone who has worked with me will tell you that I am an incredibly warm person like all Librans are and easy to work with.

Namita: On that note, let's discuss another comment you made: 'My team calls me Don.' Another one that could be misunderstood. How do you address that?

Aishwarya: Yes, I am tough on my team when needed, but this is also followed by lots of love. I have a passionate team and we are all driven by a shared vision.

Namita: You are single and I had asked you this question on the show about how you respond when people ask you stereotypical questions like, 'If you get married, will you continue this venture, will you get distracted?'

Aishwarya: These biases remain. When I get asked this question, I don't bother to reply or justify. I just laugh it off. This applies to men as well. Why is it that they don't get asked these questions! I have been told so often to show things to my dad and get his opinion. In fact, it is the other way round. He's the one who relies on my advice and opinion. At a recent entrepreneur event, there were five speakers, four men and me. My picture was at the very end. Sometimes, I wonder if this is an unconscious bias or if I am overthinking! Being a woman has been a huge strength in the skincare business. I prefer to focus on that.

Chapter 12

Leadership Mantras

'If your actions inspire others to dream more, learn more, do more and become more, you are a leader.'
—John Quincy Adams (sixth US President)

Every leader has their own unique style of leading a company, their own mantras for action and success. In this section, I wanted to cover four fundamental principles that guide me in every action and decision I take.

1. Define Your Purpose

Having a purpose that the entire organization is aligned to is extremely important. Purpose fills people with positivity, and gives them a sense of fulfillment. Purpose also is a guiding force when you are at a crossroads and need clarity for making the right decisions. As Carl Jung said, **'A true leader is always led.'** This means that their actions, decisions, and choices are always led by their unwavering vision, driven by a deep purpose. Purpose also gives you the grit and resilience to not give up when times are difficult. Clearly defining this in every organization and putting goals and timelines around it is extremely important.

At Emcure, we outline a purpose budget as a part of our annual budgeting exercise. This is not the same as a more generic broadbased CSR budget. This is specific to our initiatives in healthcare that we expect our business teams to drive. For example, we work towards awareness, detection and affordable treatment with a zest and passion that is visible top to bottom. Our dashboards measure and monitor not just the regular metrics of sales, EBITDA, attrition, etc. but also metrics defined in our purpose budget such as number of anaemia, hypertension, diabetes and bone density camps conducted, number of patients supported through discounted medicines, research grants given for important areas and many other purpose initiatives that a typical commercial MIS doesn't cover. This is also an integral part of KPIs of senior leaders and appraisals.

Purpose creates magic. At *Shark Tank India*, when the founders believed in the problem they were out to solve, passion shone in their eyes. You could sense that energy and fire in their belly. These were the founders we were most excited to partner with; the ones we most believed in.

For me, ventures that have betterment of the nation as a purpose are very important. Yes, we are objective about areas of improvement in our country but all of us believe that we need to be agents of change in our own little ways. The best way to give love back to our motherland is to work on solving various problems. This is exactly what *Shark Tank India* founders are doing! A small story to demonstrate this is that of Rajat Jain, the founder of Spandan, the home ECG device that I invested in at *Shark Tank India*. He said that most tech companies are in bigger cities and he deliberately operates out of his hometown, Dehradun. He hopes that his venture will ensure that talent from Dehradun does not have to move to bigger cities to find opportunities. Just imagine if there was a Rajat in every small town in India who created enormous job opportunities for students graduating from that city! What a beautiful nationalistic sentiment that I hope Rajat will hopefully inspire many others to follow.

Entrepreneurship is the biggest leveller in any country. It is the best way to democratize wealth creation. It ensures that high net worth is not just the prerogative of those born with a silver spoon in their mouth but also those who dare to dream. It is a huge incentive and motivation for the country's youth. Brain drain is a serious concern in our country and entrepreneurship is the best way to counter that. When youngsters see opportunity and role models in the start-up ecosystem, and successful exits in the forms of IPOs and acquisitions, that's when we will see more start-ups.

2. Less Is More

This is probably the most important line that has guided me in every decision I have made. For example, at

Emcure, let's look at the evolution of the new launches policy. There was a time when we would launch a large number of brands to get the medical reps excited, and create buzz in the doctor's chambers. That was until I saw large supply chain issues, expiry and low growth in key brands. I realized new launches were a distraction from making big brands bigger. Narrow your focus by reducing new launches and double down on your big brands! The day I executed this strategy, my sales and brand building scaled newer heights. At *Shark Tank India*, we saw this so often. Founders had barely started and had already launched more SKUs than they could handle. As is always the case, 80 per cent of sales would come from 20 per cent of products but the balance products would drain resources and time. This was the most common and repeated feedback from Sharks to the founders.

3. Hire Teams Smarter Than You

A secure leader will always hire teams that are smarter than them; teams that challenge the leader and are open to dissent. Then you empower them, be a coach when needed and watch the magic happen. Many leaders want yes-people. Smart teams will not do that! This insecurity in leaders deprives the venture of talented professionals who can add so much value. Smart teams need to be given equity, and made to feel that sense of ownership. Again, this is not easy to part with but absolutely essential to bring talent in. Often, at *Shark Tank India*, when Sharks saw glaring functional weaknesses in the business, mostly in technology and marketing, the founders were advised to share equity and get a domain expert as a co-founder. The advice was to basically put a strong team in place to help the business gain credibility and scale. At Emcure, we saw the full glory and power of this leadership mantra during the COVID lockdown. Since pharmaceuticals were essential services, we were at our offices all through the lockdown. Our primary job was to ensure that there were no shortages of medicines pan India. The way our leaders ensured that workers showed up despite the paranoia was magical. Manufacturing was seamless, distribution happened pan India despite huge challenges and all our sales reps visited doctors to deliver PPE kits and masks at a time when they were barely available. We had hired great teams and empowered them and we saw first hand how these teams got going and made things happen during the pandemic.

4. Execution Is Paramount

Strategy is good but flawless and rigorous execution is what builds large businesses. Execution is a balancing act between agility that a start-up has vs the systems, SOPs and governance that are needed for scaling organizations. SOPs and governance structures put in a culture of attention to detail but this must be balanced with entrepreneurial agility, sense of urgency and action bias that made you a successful start-up to begin with. Most start-ups at *Shark Tank India* were pre-revenue or small revenue and during due diligence, many were difficult to navigate for us as investors. They did not have their accounts in order, and several tax and secretarial non-compliance issues had to be sorted before we invested our money. Start-ups need to be educated on these basics and their importance.

A few ventures that sounded great on paper missed out on deals due to execution lapses. I was very interested in the diabetes device, Vivalyf, till Peyush's reading during the pitch turned out to be inaccurate. Similarly, I am a big believer in Ayurveda and wanted to invest in the app AyuRythm till they tested me and told me my 'prakriti' was pitta when I very well know that for years, I have been 'vata prakriti'. At Emcure, I worked on making the sales team culture more planning and detail oriented. Just by ensuring that events and tour plans are scheduled in advance and not last minute, we took the EBITDA up several notches. It sounds so small and simple but to get this done with 5000 medical reps was a test of our commitment to execution. Similarly, when one of our newly launched brands, Dydrofem, failed, we took it up as a challenge. Through a flawless execution on three levers—pan India science meets, creative in-clinic campaigns and innovative incentive structures, we turned around the brand and made it one of our top selling brands this year. Very often, execution is nothing but the discipline and consistency in doing everyday small things right.

Every founder has their own journey, their own unique style, battles and learnings. One final thought that I would like to leave the readers with is that leadership is not a popularity contest. In fact, most often, leadership is about ignoring the noise around and staying true to your core convictions and beliefs. As my favorite quote on leadership goes, '**To lead an orchestra, you must turn your back on the crowd.**'

Interaction with Supam Maheshwari, Co-Founder and CEO, FirstCry.com

Supam is the quintessential entrepreneur—focused on his work—and is rarely seen at public or corporate events or on social media. Where is the time for this? This Pune-based serial entrepreneur has built four start-ups (three of them being unicorns) in twelve years! Brainvisa, which got acquired in 2009; FirstCry, which redefined the baby care industry in India; XpressBees, which was hived off from FirstCry and is a delivery company and, finally GlobalBees, which is a Thrasio-style brand aggregator. It gives me so much joy to be acquainted with a brilliant entrepreneur who has built all these out of my city, Pune. I had a chat with Supam to get insights into the rarely seen or heard entrepreneur, how he thinks, what is his vision and how he has been a pioneer and original thinker in so many ways in the D2C space!

Leadership Style and Mantras That Helped Him Create and Scale Multiple Businesses

There are three areas that Supam is very particular about. They are: hiring the right people, inculcating a strong execution focused team culture and always leading by example to create potential leaders for tomorrow. In terms of hiring, his companies have had negative attrition in the senior team as people believed in the vision that they have collectively defined and delivered on. In fact, many have joined hands again from Brainvisa days even after it got acquired. In terms of hiring, Supam always looks for attitude over competence. Early on in his journey, he had a painful episode that taught him the importance of doing so. While building Brainvisa, he was travelling a lot to the US for business development. He had hired a sales head from one of his competitors and found out that this person had not only started his own company on the side but was also diverting business from Brainvisa clients at company expense! Supam believes competency can be taught but attitude cannot. Without a great attitude, you can never build a team that you can trust blindly. Once you have a competent leadership team on whom you have blind trust/ faith, that defines your core team and foundation. This is a huge must to ensure a sustainable and high bar of continued success. These team members are groomed very carefully with the right culture of no politics, no ego and pure meritocracy and thereby go on to become ambassadors of hiring further like-minded team members and building great institutions.

Supam is very detail-oriented. He still gets a hundred reports a day and is known to ask questions five levels down to get to the bottom of things. For example, customer feedback is very critical for him and if he sees a wrong order that has gone to a customer, he will even watch CCTV footage to see whether this is a mistake at the packaging line or elsewhere. He likes to get to the root of the problem to instill the right culture. He is very patient in coaching and nurturing when the first mistake happens but his team knows that he will not be so accommodating of the same mistake the second time. This builds a culture of 100 per cent accuracy and excellence. It all starts from the leader being hands-on and asking right and tough questions and building a great execution team. While he is a macro manager, his team will also tell you that he is equally a micro manager and if one wants to see him rattled, one needs to mess with that. That's when he won't sleep and won't let anyone else sleep till it is resolved or hasn't reached a satisfactory level. The leadership team DNA of both XpressBees and GlobalBees reflects the same ethos as described above and allows them to scale immensely.

Origin of XpressBees and GlobalBees and Allocating Time to Competing Priorities

Supam, along with three co-founders, started his entrepreneurial journey at Brainvisa, an education company that provided consumer education. But they were ahead of their time. That didn't work out, so they pivoted to becoming an enterprise eLearning company in the B2B space. However, they decided to sell it at a good value as consulting businesses generate good profits but tend to plateau and they did not see any further scope for scaling it.

Then came FirstCry which has been a phenomenal journey and subsequently the evolution of GlobalBees, a natural extension of FirstCry.

FirstCry started its journey by being an online marketplace for products for newborn babies and kids. They built several big brands on this platform. However, they are most proud of BabyHug, a homegrown brand.

They call it a home brand and not a private label as private label seems like a narrow term that is merely focused on margins. BabyHug has become the largest baby and kids brand and sells everything from personal care products like diapers, shampoos, oils, lotions, and diaper creams to big-ticket items like car seats and strollers. It has a wide range of fashion and foot wear products as well. Today, BabyHug probably has the largest product assortment in the baby/kids space in the entire world. It is a mass premium brand that has earned trust, and is synonymous with quality and reliability in mothers' minds.

Over time, he believes they have cracked nuances of building great D2C brands using digital marketing, influencer marketing, community engagement, product positioning, packaging, and using data analytics effectively to tweak their customer strategies. They have built a solid global supply chain and understand what works and how to execute it. So they decided to start GlobalBees to acquire smaller brands in the D2C space and use their established and proven playbook to help these consumer brands scale. It was a natural extension of FirstCry and made sense.

XpressBees also has an interesting rationale, emanating from its association with the mother company, FirstCry. Back in the day, the company did not have too many reliable delivery options. So, they started their own in-house delivery service to solve this. Over time, to fill loads, they started taking third-party orders too and realized that they were fulfilling a large unmet need for efficiency and reliability. Within a short period of this success and scale, they hived off this business. It took time to convince investors since investors always think that founders are doing too many things and will meet with execution hazards and increase their risk. Today, with great execution, it is one of the top two e-commerce delivery providers in the country.

The Battle between Founder Ideology, Vision and the Investor's Mindset

For start-ups, managing investors is a critical task. While he is always grateful for the capital and trust of investors and wants them to get exponential returns, at times, since many investors don't have operational experience, Supam thinks it is tough for them to see a founder's unique vision. They tend to get caught up in short-term IRR (internal rate of return) expectations, expediting the safety net of next round and overall, getting trapped into a herd mentality, especially in businesses which are very early. One instance where they had a tough time with investors is when they felt strongly about going omnichannel. No one had done this before so it was all new and tough for people to fully grasp. What made Supam confident that this would work for them was when they put two facts together in 2010— one, even after 5–10 years, 90 per cent consumers were still shopping offline, and second, there were no visible scaled-up players in the baby and kids space other than a couple that were much smaller. They convinced investors that they would implement an offline channel while, at the same time, addressing and respecting two key investor concerns: investor money should not be used for this exercise and that Supam's time should not be diverted for this. They solved for this by opting for a franchise model for their offline strategy. Of all places, their first franchise was from an over-enthusiastic gentleman who approached them from Bharuch, Gujarat! Since then, they haven't looked back and scaled pan India. Supam feels proud that they pioneered omnichannel retailing in this country. Now, this omnichannel strategy is almost a given for all consumer brands and no one raises any doubts and concerns anymore.

Picking Pune as His Headquarters Twenty Years Ago, though It Was Not the Most Preferred Hub for Entrepreneurs

Supam moved to Pune twenty-two years ago as his wife is from the city and since then, has never left the city or felt the need to. Right from Brainvisa to FirstCry to XpressBees, all his ventures have been headquartered here. He did face initial challenges in getting tech talent but then, they trained their team and additionally, good talent also moved from different cities to join them in Pune. Quite a few employees from Brainvisa have gone on to create meaningful entrepreneurial ventures and he is very proud of them. Their first warehouse was in Pune. In a consumer business, suppliers find you and in that sense, your location does not matter. He cites examples of Walmart and Albertsons in the USA. They were founded in smaller cities. He loves the climate, the culture, and being in Pune has worked out very well for him and his companies.

Vision Going Forward

Their legal counsels have strictly guided them not to say much on this as they have plans of going public in the near future. However, Supam says that they run a tight ship and are happy that they have been profitable for a while. He believes it is very important to be focused on fundamentals and execution. Supam's vision is to be the leader in the 'mother-baby-kids' ecosystem in India and other select geographies that they plan to go after. They launched in the Middle East a year ago and are already the market leaders there. This gives them the confidence that they can scale and achieve a dominant position in other countries as well. The sky is the limit!

Chapter 13

The 3Cs of Entrepreneurship

Every founder deserves respect for stepping out of their comfort zone and undertaking a journey that does not guarantee success but is one that is fraught with more setbacks, sacrifices, sweat, blood and tears than one signs up for.

About 62,000 entrepreneurs applied and we got to see 198 of them at *Shark Tank India*. A lot has been written about what skills an entrepreneur must have but below are the 3Cs that I believe are essential.

Courage

Aristotle says, **'Courage is the first of human qualities because it is the quality that guarantees others.'** It takes courage to be an entrepreneur, to stand by your convictions and go the long haul with a venture you believe in! Calculated risk taking is one of the most important skills needed and courage ensures this. It also makes sure you continue in spite of several naysayers and non-believers. It ensures grit and resilience.

After ten years in Emcure as the CFO, it took courage for me to step out of my comfort zone and head the India business, an area I had no prior experience in. It came with its complexity of brand building, managing a large field force and cultural nuances in sales teams with larger egos and expectations. I had more than my share of moments of self-doubt. This combined with road blocks by old-timers and interference by my well-meaning father, made the going very tough in the initial two years. I worked hard at learning by doing. I talked to industry experts, sat for hours with the in-house medical and research teams to understand our products, and interacted with doctors and trade. It took guts to bring massive leadership changes, and new systems and cultural changes while at the same time not losing focus on building sales and profitability. Nothing worthwhile is ever achieved without mustering the courage to step outside your comfort zone and that's exactly what happened in this case. Ghalib rightly says, '*Manzil milegi bhatak kar hi sahi, gumrah toh who hain joh ghar se nikle hi nahi.*' (Fortune favours the brave.)

Similarly, I remember the story of Duvvuru Varshitha of the venture, Vivalyf at *Shark Tank India*. She got into research and didn't pursue a corporate career as she wanted to start early and dedicate her life to finding a painless solution to detecting diabetes. This non-invasive diabetes testing device will take years to get validated and approved and may not even see the light of the day. But despite a cluttered market, and a slew of MNCs out to do the same and meagre resources, she set out to keep the promise she made to her father. This is fearlessness at another level! But courage has to be backed by strong logic and market research. In the venture Julaa at *Shark Tank India* (automated swing for children) the three founders had put in Rs 25 lakh in a prototype without any sound market research on customer insights, competitors and pricing. This is not the right type of courage needed for an entrepreneur. Like I had said in that episode, '*Umeed aur sales ka faasla bahut lamba hota hai.*' (There is a long journey to be traversed between mere hope and actual sales.)

Competence

You need to live and breathe your venture. You need to become a domain expert to another level. Do you always need an IIT or IIM degree to make it big? Sure, a structured degree and way of thinking always helps but haven't we all seen entrepreneurs without these who have made us proud? In business, competence is established by results and sales, and not merely degrees. I remember working hard to become a CA at twenty-one years and then being the first girl from my family to go to the US to get a degree (MBA). But when I moved back to join my dad's business, those degrees and six years of work experience in the US meant absolutely nothing. I had to start from scratch to gain trust, respect and establish my credibility. My competence was established by my results, outcomes and sales, not my degrees.

At *Shark Tank India*, I preferred companies with some revenue instead of pre-revenue. It wasn't because I was playing it safe. It was due to my strong belief that a market launch, hard knocks and learnings post launch are the only things that establish credibility, product-market fit and make an entrepreneur truly a domain expert. At *Shark Tank India*, there was an interesting venture called Sabji Kothi, which increased the shelf life of fruits and vegetables through a uniquely designed fruit cart that needed only 10 watts of electricity. This is an important problem to solve for the farmers of our country and the founder was a PhD in design from IIT Kanpur. He asked for a valuation of Rs 24 crore. However, he had not launched the product and did not have customer insights and data that would give us that comfort. In this case, being pre-revenue and not having market validation hurt his prospects of getting funding from any Shark.

Compassion

Every entrepreneur must be driven by a higher purpose, a deep-rooted need to solve a problem. Compassionate leaders are effectively able to communicate this purpose-driven mindset to their teams and create a culture of empathy. Such empathy helps in retaining and motivating key talent. Altor Helmets set out with a mission to reduce road accidents, driven by their personal experience of a close friend's death. Thinkerbell set out to increase literacy in the blind population globally. AAS Vidyalaya believed in a dream, where through their edtech venture, all kids would pass the tenth grade. Education, especially in the interiors and rural areas, has had a massive setback due to the pandemic. Children without tablets, phones and electricity have dropped out and this has set the country back by several years. In case of AAS Vidyalaya, the passion to make a difference in this space shone in their eyes!

Compassion also ensures that you stay humble and this, in turn, ensures you listen to others with respect and continue to be a lifelong student. Compassion ensures you see the problems your employees and end users face more clearly. A brilliant case in point is that of Satya Nadella of Microsoft. There are many articles around how he transformed the toxic and overly competitive environment at Microsoft once he took over. He credits this turnaround to him having more compassion because he was a father to a child with cerebral palsy. Unfortunately, Zain passed away in early 2022 at the age of twenty-six.

Another great example of a leader with compassion is Harsh Mariwala of Marico. He is one of India's most reputed business leaders. In addition to Marico, he has invested his time and resources in three areas that will have a strong social impact. The first is Ascent Foundation. It creates a close-knit trust group of non-competing entrepreneurs who believe in peer learning by sharing experiences, ideas and insights in a safe, confidential and non-judgemental environment. Second is the Mariwala Health Initiative which provides grants and strategic support to organizations working with communities to provide greater access to mental health services. Finally, Marico Innovation Foundation that helps innovative start-ups scale by providing them operational support and also gives out awards and monetary grants for such innovative start-ups. In addition, even his Venture Fund, Sharrp

Ventures, has a strong inclination towards funding start-ups with innovation and social impact at their core.

Courage, competence and compassion can help you deal with the innumerable failures that are part of every entrepreneur's journey. Failure is still considered a taboo in our country. It is condemned and not celebrated. Why? It can be the best teacher if we embrace it and keep an open mind. Like Oprah Winfrey says, so beautifully, **'Whenever you have a setback, ask yourself the right question. Not why is this happening to me, but what is this here to teach me.'** It puts you in the place and space to get the lesson you need. It's all these failures, and the humiliation that teach and build so much character, so much empathy and help you enjoy success, when it comes, with so much more gratitude and joy!

I wish we can teach this to all our kids early on in life. When I started Thapar Entrepreneurs Academy, six years back, the students who would not get funded at our investor panel would feel very demotivated. Their parents would call us to question why their teen didn't make it to the top three rankings. This demonstrated to me how deep-rooted this taboo is, in our culture. Parents and kids weren't focused on what they had learned through the six months but rather on that three-minute pitch and rank which they felt defined them! I hope we all have the courage to have a better attitude and reaction when we encounter failures and setbacks in life.

At *Shark Tank India*, we saw entrepreneurs who displayed so much courage, competence and compassion. I thought I would teach them something, but they taught me a lot more. They inspired me, moved me and their lessons and stories will motivate me for life!

Here's an interview with Ranodeep Saha from *Shark Tank India* who truly demonstrates all of the above qualities that I deeply admire. I am proud to be part of his journey! His venture, Rare Planet, sells Indian handicrafts.

Namita: Rano, I am so proud that you are working towards reviving Indian art and augmenting the livelihoods of artists in India. Such a fantastic purpose. When did you start this and how is Rare Planet enabling this?

Rano: I'm from Kolkata and most Bengali children are taught painting. Art is an integral part of our childhood. I have always grown up with a love for art and painting. When I saw next-generation karigars not wanting to continue their traditions, I felt the need to do something about this. I realized that one of the biggest challenges is that everything is handmade and this makes it difficult to standardize and scale. I hired an NIFT graduate and a consultant from NID and worked on developing more scientific manufacturing methods which exponentially increased the productivity and earning potential of karigars. It is only when you make this a lucrative and sustainable profession that the next generation would want to continue it. As of today, Rare Planet supports 2000 karigars directly and 10,000 indirectly, and this is just the beginning.

Namita: Rano, most of your workforce is women and you work actively towards their empowerment. Tell us more about that.

Rano: Most often, a *parivar* (family) of karigars gets associated with me and I always ensure that I open a bank account for the woman of the household and deposit the income in her name. This ensures that the earnings are used well and saved or spent for the right reasons. This is something very close to my heart as my mother has been my biggest support and inspiration. Empowering women is something that she and I both want to work towards.

Namita: What is your vision for Rare Planet going forward?

Rano: I have provided jobs to many karigars and as I scale, this number will increase. But the key point here is how do I help them scale too. I have a plan for this. I want to work with a fintech company to provide loans to the karigars so that they can scale and help us grow too. Just like there is a Chanel or Louis Vuitton store on every high-end street in world's largest cities, I dream of a day when I can showcase India's rich heritage through Rare Planet stores that will have a place of pride alongside these very stores!

Namita: What has been the biggest success story of your entrepreneurial journey?

Rano: When I was in ninth grade, my father lost all his money due to his capital being stuck in goods that were impacted with anti-dumping duty, a new regulation that no one had seen coming. We had to sell our factory, home, car, and pretty much everything we owned. It was very painful. All of us, including me, started doing odd jobs to support the family income. I remember taking tuitions and painting kulhads that I would sell at school fests. These tough times built the drive in me. I had a deep desire to help my parents regain at least some of what they had lost. Rare Planet has done well and I recently secured a loan to buy a small home for my parents. This has been the biggest high point of my journey so far!

Chapter 14

The Vulnerable Leader

Leaders are always expected to be Type A, show aggression and be in control. Several TV shows, books and movies that have portrayed the quintessential tycoon have reinforced this Alpha male/female image of a leader in our minds. This is changing. Today, in a world that is vying for scarce talent, employees gravitate towards companies driven by a purpose and leaders who are grounded, and unafraid to show their vulnerabilities and talk openly about their failures. Business speeches and motivational talks are more appreciated when they are personal and talking about setbacks and painful journeys. That's what makes leaders relatable and inspiring. It's the humility, and the authenticity which comes with the comfort of showing one's vulnerable side.

Advantages for Leaders Showing Their Vulnerability

1. **Vulnerability is the ultimate courage**: Many misunderstand vulnerability to be a sign of weakness,

a sign that others will take you for a ride, a sign that you are not capable of being an aggressive outcome-driven leader. It's exactly the opposite. It takes enormous courage to show your flaws, your insecurities and courage is the most important trait that builds trust and respect for a leader.

2. **Culture of empathy**: We all spend most of our time at our workplaces. We want to be surrounded by people who are authentic, and in a space where it is ok to not posture and alright to let our guard down. A place where vulnerability is looked at as a strength breeds a culture of compassion. It is ok to be flawed and to be 'human'. This promotes candour. Imagine if you had to posture and pose for eight hours a day. It is exhausting and drains your energy. Vulnerable leaders bring out positive and productive bests in their teams.

3. **Culture of creativity and innovation**: Innovation takes place when people are willing to step out of their comfort zones, to take risks and, when they are not afraid to fail. They don't feel judged and labelled. They know they will not be laughed at or looked down upon. They feel like they are in a psychological safe zone and feel comfortable discussing their failures. When the leader sets the example by doing exactly this, the team follows and this leads to creativity and the most innovative outcomes.

I am not afraid to talk about my mistakes, and judgement errors openly in meetings and town halls. This rawness and honesty often gives my team the courage to try new things, even if there is no guarantee of success, simply because they are secure in the knowledge that there will not be any job loss or humiliation as long as they are competent and have made a sincere effort. For example, we had a leader who did not do well in a sales role but had very good doctor relationships and thrived in a line function like market research. There are enough and more of these examples at Emcure, that make it comfortable for people to keep trying, knowing that if they are good and still fail, that's ok. They know that there will be patient leaders who will help them find a better fit for their talents, thus creating a win-win for them and the company.

When you are afraid to be vulnerable, to feel and express pain, then you project your pain onto people by calling your insecurities as theirs, by labelling and judging them, and by pigeonholing them.

I would like to give some examples of how people got labelled and judged and demotivated at *Shark Tank India* and how damaging that was to some of the founders and their self-esteem. I would then like to give examples of moments when I showed vulnerability and how scary that was at first, but then, how much at peace I felt, and how I used it at work and in my various talks to give hope to others. It truly felt empowering!

Labelling at *Shark Tank India*
Sharks Got Labelled

At *Shark Tank India*, each Shark has scaled businesses which obviously involved tremendous business acumen and an all-round understanding of various functional areas combined with a high EQ to build the right leadership team. Yet, we all ended Season One with labels. Aman, the branding guru. Peyush, the technology expert. Namita, the healthcare lady who is biased towards women entrepreneurs. Vineeta, the D2C brand builder. Anupam, the seasoned investor who has invested in start-ups for over ten years. Ashneer, the finance expert and Ghazal, the lady with a love for sustainability. Our memes reinforced a lot of these labels! I found that quite strange given we are all business experts and not specific domain experts.

Even founders came in with specific preferences as to which Shark they wanted based on these labels for us in their mind. For example, the EV start-up, Revamp Moto and the undergarment venture, Bummer, had come in thinking that they needed a marketing expert like Aman and therefore, rejected Ashneer's offer even though he has also built brands and offered a better valuation than Aman did.

Founders Got Labelled

Some of the common feedback given at *Shark Tank India* labelled founders as weak in marketing (your packaging isn't good/brand name isn't good/you need a marketing co-founder) or weak in technology (your user interface isn't good enough/you need a technology co-founder).

I would like to narrate one pitch where the extent of labelling bothered me so much that after the pitch, I had to rush to my vanity van so that I didn't blow up! Anyone who knows me could tell from my face how disturbed I was at the way feedback was provided during the pitch.

The start-up in question was Good Good Piggy, the fintech brand from Episode 14. I am ok with the fact that investors did not find the business good enough to invest in and recommended that she shut it down. Feedback is important and useful as long as it's not personal and humiliating.

What I didn't appreciate are the personal allegations made at the founder such as:

- When she tried to promote herself through her achievements such as 'woman in tech ambassa-dor', she was told that she was using too many jargons and this was not impressing anybody. Why shouldn't she use these achievements to promote herself? She was told that she used terms like UN, Paris and Geneva to answer questions. We haven't even heard of these places was the comment. Is such sarcasm warranted?

- She was asked to talk about progress she has made in our country. When she spoke about work done in Sundar Nursery, she was told that Sundar Nursery was a place where rich people go for picnics. Nobody talks about work there. Can we run down any place in this manner?

- She was told that investors understand neither English nor jargon. They have built businesses from scratch. By merely speaking and reading English, you cannot build a business. When she refuted that she has done ground work, she was asked how could she possibly do this by twenty-five? Why not?

Is a twenty-minute interaction enough for you to judge a person and write their obituary on national television to such an extent? Possibly my co-Sharks had her best interest at heart and felt this candour would help her but there is always a thin line between helpful feedback and humiliation. I personally felt that this line was crossed at times.

Guilty as Charged

Was I personally guilty of such harsh judgement and labelling, and did I slip as well? Absolutely yes. I am a strong believer that even if we choose not to invest in a venture, we must respect the entrepreneur, and respect the fact that they chose this path full of setbacks and difficulties. I disrespected an entrepreneur and felt pretty ashamed of myself for doing so.

The Sharks were invited on the hugely popular Indian comedy show called *The Kapil Sharma Show*. When the seven Sharks were asked by Kapil if there was any crazy pitch that stood out in our minds, I was the first to respond by saying 'the belly button shaper' was the craziest and worst pitch! To act funny and cool, I made fun of an entrepreneur. What gives me the right to do that? It may have been an unrealistic and unviable idea to me, but here is a middle-class couple who had poured their life savings and efforts into this venture that they whole-heartedly believed in. Yes, as well-meaning experts, it's very much within our right to objectively guide them on why this is not viable by explaining the constraints in very clear terms. But to single them out and laugh at them on national television is something that is unacceptable and something that I will always be ashamed of.

As Khalil Gibran said, '**To belittle, you have to be little.**'

Some labels are deliberate and helpful. Brand managers for products and celebrities spend crores on labelling them to fit a certain look and niche. That is ok. It is part of doing business. Where it is not ok is when it limits someone from reaching their growth and full potential like we do when we recklessly label our children or our employees or when it hurts someone's feelings with no value-add. Labels limit and cripple most. Very few can get thick-skinned, rise above these labels and have the grit and self-belief to keep pursuing their goals. If we cannot help someone, let's at least not handicap them by labelling them. We need to lift and not label.

My Experience with Labelling

I wanted to talk candidly about a few labels that I personally acquired over the thirty-six episodes.

Yeh meri expertise nahi hai (I am not an expert in this).

Putting yourself in the public eye opens you up to merciless trolling. I got so many comments stating that if I don't invest in a venture saying I am not an expert, then I don't deserve a seat on *Shark Tank India*. I must admit that it initially really got to me. I felt humiliated that in spite of two degrees like CA and MBA and twenty-plus years of work experience, I was made to feel like I was inadequate and not good enough to be an investor on the show! Negative moments can either make you bitter and paralyze you or make you better and help you evolve. I am glad I chose the latter.

I realized that it takes a lot of humility to accept that you don't know enough in an area and choose to opt out as you can't add value. I am proud that I had the authenticity to do so. It takes a lot of self-discipline and maturity to say 'NO'. It is easy to get carried away when you are shooting for fourteen hours a day and say 'yes' to deals for all the wrong reasons. I had the best interest of the founders at heart. I could easily pretend to know something but I genuinely wanted the founders to get the best investor in terms of someone who would be able to help them scale much more than I could. Once I made peace with that and thought it through, I used this as my tag line in several social media posts and speeches. Trust me, this always gets the audience to crack up and makes me look like the superhero!

Namita Doesn't Know Technology

This social media trolling didn't get to me. In fact, I found it quite amusing. Founders are tech experts anyway. They need someone who can guide them with the business side of things, marketing, finance, and distribution. Someone who can help them scale and help them go global, all of which I understand and have done.

Namita Is Not a Founder

I find this the most entertaining; the girl with the silver spoon label. Second generations work mighty hard to innovate, infuse new perspectives and solid systems, all of which help to scale the business. You need an absolutely entrepreneurial mindset to launch new brands and divisions within an older setting to take the company to the next level. There were remarks like 'she has old money', 'she probably never had to deal with having no funds in her bank account'. Do they even know about the childhood I had where we, as a family, dealt with a lot of this and more as my father struggled financially and how it scarred me as a teenager? People judge, people label, people assume all the time. It's best to just smile and let them think what they want to think.

The One Time I Really Slipped

But here, I must confess that as thick-skinned as I would like to believe I am, I let the negative talk get to me. For those who saw the exclusive and final episode #36 on Sony Liv, you will notice that I got defensive. I lost clarity of thought, and I was out to prove some labels wrong. I wasn't thinking straight. I made offers to four of the five pitchers that day, more to prove a point rather than do the right thing. I lost my authenticity. When Aman, in his sweet and well-meaning candid style, pointed it out to me in private, I ferociously disagreed with him rather than mulling over it and accepting it. Days later, when the episode released, I was shocked to see myself and couldn't believe some of the things I had said. That wasn't the real me! The final nail in the coffin was when my mother sent me long and scathing WhatsApp messages. That's when it hit me—how I had let the opinions of others kill my authenticity. I learned my lesson and swore to work harder at strengthening my core and not let any such labels get to me in the future.

One More Label from My Teen Years

I was overweight as a teenager. I was body shamed which led to low self-esteem. There was incredible family pressure to stand first in class, and be a board ranker which led to severe anxiety and depression in my teens. All these labels deprived me of a fun childhood; years that I should have spent being curious, exploring new concepts, and having fun with friends, I was too busy crying over labels and judging myself based on others' expectations. But this phase built character and helped me get my strongest quality as a leader—empathy.

I want to share how I used it effectively. My YouTube show on women's health, 'Uncondition Yourself' was a project very close to my heart. I interviewed doctors and women to share their journeys, their pain and their triumphs. During 2–3 episodes, I was in a dilemma as there was social pressure not to talk about my experiences with depression, body shaming and two failed infertility treatments.

But ultimately, I spoke about them all. My biggest reason was to inspire hope in others, to normalize these conditions, and most importantly, to show that no one's life is perfect, no matter what you like to believe. As a leader, am I better off showing my perfect life or am I better off using the power of my voice to talk about uncomfortable topics and taboos and to create awareness about these issues? If showing my flaws made many watching the show feel better about themselves and gave them strength, it was mission accomplished.

When you really step back and analyze, you see that to a large extent, social media and our obsession with it has contributed to this need for labelling, and showing our lives as perfect . . . that perfect vacation, the perfect surprise gift given by your doting husband, beautiful children, awards, etc. As a consequence, we hesitate from showing our vulnerabilities and imperfections.

The day I made my peace with these labels and used them to my advantage as a leader, I was unstoppable. I started talking about it at work, in my talks, in my writings, on social media and the love I got for it was so incredible.

When business leaders get called for speeches, people talk about being inspired by their achievements. Their resumes read out at these events are super long and glittery, filled with awards and accolades. I dream of a day when we introduce ourselves not just through our achievements but also through our flaws. When our talks are as much about our failures and insecurities as they are about our accomplishments, for this is what truly influences and inspires.

Interview with Sagar Daryani, Co-Founder and CEO, Wow! Momos

I met Sagar through a common friend, his investor, Rochelle Dsouza from Lighthouse Funds. He had never met me in person but graciously agreed to host a field trip at one of his Mumbai restaurants for students of my entrepreneurship academy. Not only did he spend time interacting with all of them but he was also the most generous host and spoiled them with trays of wow foods, gift vouchers and a book by Elon Musk for each and every student.

This generosity, empathy and positive spirit really touched my heart and has stayed with me since then. Again, it was sheer destiny that I invested in a company at *Shark Tank India*, Rare Planet. Rano, the founder, is Sagar's mentee and Rare Planet happens to be Sagar's very first investment as an angel investor. We reconnected after a gap of three years. It was a sign and I felt that I had to cover his story in this book.

When I interviewed him, what touched my heart the most is when he revealed his vulnerability and spoke openly about his mental health issues. That's when I felt strongly that his story should be as much about his fantastic professional achievements as his painful personal struggles; struggles, which in his own words, made him a better leader in many ways. This chapter seemed like the perfect fit for his story. But let's first start with his fantastic journey as an entrepreneur. In this interview, you will find stories that reflect the essence of many chapters, right from courage of the 3Cs to how he has used the power of networking to being an excellent mentor. A man with many dimensions and a heart that's just WOW!

Namita: Sagar, you come from a business family. Why didn't you join the family business?

Sagar: My father had a retail garment business. I saw first hand how local stores and unorganized players like him suffered from the advent of the mall culture. This is when I understood the power of brand building. Around then, I was in college and hugely inspired by

'Momo Aunty' whose momos we absolutely loved. I wanted to be a part of the food industry, an industry that builds an emotional connect with consumers; that is an integral part of their daily social lives, a part of their important milestones and celebrations. I wanted to experience that!

Many well-meaning relatives and neighbours dissuaded my father from helping me, saying that I was wasting my education by selling momos which are a 'low class product' but my father never mentioned this to me once. On the contrary, my parents have been my biggest support system, my truest mentors!

Namita: You started this business with Rs 30,000 cash and today, you have Rs 600 crore sales, 500 stores, 4000 employees and marquee investors like IAN, Lighthouse and Tiger Global. You have built a strong homegrown brand in a category where no one thought they could compete with the likes of KFC or Burger King! Congratulations! Let's talk about brand building. What has been your vision, your biggest differentiator?

Sagar: I always wanted to create a fun brand. My differentiator was that the momo market, till then, had two primary products—the vegetarian momo that was full of cabbage and the non-vegetarian chicken option which was more onion and less chicken. I saw a huge opportunity to innovate with flavours. We introduced Indian versions like paneer momos, corn and cheese momos, prawn and fish momos, and butter chicken momos. We had the fried and steamed versions; and we came up with interesting dip options, especially the green dhaniya dip among others. We branched out to momo burgers and momo sizzlers and even introduced dessert options like chocolate momos. We constantly work with analytics to figure out patterns and trends which helps us decide what to add to our menu and most importantly, what to remove from it. Another aspect we worked on was the quality—we made the skin thinner, and the size larger. We basically studied all the gaps in the market and that helped us innovate and come up with a differentiated range.

We used this expertise and success mantra to build Wow! Chicken and Wow! China. Taking KFC head-on with Wow! Chicken was a big bet we took. When we said we would offer chicken that was 0 per cent MSG and with no chicken skin, people didn't think this health angle would take off. But this differentiator, along with an innovative Indianized menu, was a huge hit. Today, I can proudly say that our store may be one-fourth the size of KFC but has 50 per cent revenue of an average KFC store. Now that we have cracked this, we are ready to expand aggressively pan India! We also expanded into the frozen packaged food category. We worked with food consultants from Japan, Taiwan and Italy and invested in R&D to ensure our momos tasted fresh even without preservatives. We worked hard on increasing the shelf life of momos from two days to ninety days. Though COVID hit around that time and everyone including our investors asked us to delay the launch, I still went ahead and today, this packaged food category has also been a huge success. I personally work on everything right from t-shirts that our employees wear to their training to quality standards. We want to create a 'Made in India' brand that we can truly be proud of. I dream of a day I can boast of a large momo factory and can take my brand global!

Namita: Currently, your QSR business is 50 per cent of your sales and online sales brings about 50 per cent. Was this a conscious strategy from the very beginning?

Sagar: Actually, this is a great case study of how adversity can break you or bring out the best in you. We had a brilliant run all the way from inception in 2008 to 2020. I often say that it felt like a 'blockbuster Bollywood' movie. Then came COVID in April 2020, when our sales reduced by 90 per cent. We had never seen any losses and in April alone, we had Rs 6 crore in losses. We had to adapt quickly, and that's when we innovated again. Our delivery business, which was only 20 per cent at the time, had to be ramped up. Momos are not a delivery-friendly product, so we had to innovate our packaging with foil inside to ensure that the momos stayed warm, firm and did not break yet retained their freshness. We curated the menu to make it more delivery-friendly, and pivoted to having cloud kitchens pan India. As a result, in the second wave, our business was down just 25 per cent vs 90 per cent in the first wave. We were happy that we had finally created a COVID-proof business but this opened our eyes to the enormous opportunity of a phygital (online and offline) business model! COVID helped us think of other new ways to innovate.

We started momo carts in Café Coffee Day outlets, started having a mix of Wow! Momos and Wow! China offerings in the same restaurant to optimize space and to optimize local deliveries. All these new initiatives have augmented our bottom line while building scale. So COVID was a game changer for our business strategy and outlook.

Namita: You are a big believer in the power of networks. Tell us more about how you have cultivated networks and how this has helped you personally and professionally?

Sagar: I want to give two examples of networks. First is how I raised my first round of funding. Trade associations and conferences are a great place for start-ups to create networks with peers, vendors, customers as well as investors. I was a regular at such conferences and association meets. In 2011, I pitched at a TiE business plan competition in Kolkata. I did not prepare and the very first pitch of my life was not an impressive one by any standards. But I still managed to pique the interest of Indian Angel Network who offered me Rs 2.5 crore at a Rs 10 crore valuation. I didn't accept the funding as I panicked after reading the complex legal terms like drag on and tag along among others. I didn't have a team and I didn't think I would be able to meet their expectations in terms of growth and scale. I was honestly scared and refused the money but this network taught me a lot about the concept of angel funding.

In 2015, when I had expanded to forty-three stores, Rs 10 crore in sales (completely bootstrapped) and had a good team in place, I attended TiE Con again. I had set up a Wow! Momo stall and this is where I met Sanjeev Bikhchandani who was intrigued that there was a larger line at my stall than the free five-star food being served at the conference. He tried my momos and loved the taste. We had dinner together and he was sold on my venture. He worked with IAN to lead the largest angel round in India and I was offered Rs 10 crore at a Rs 100 crore valuation this time! Ninety-six investors participated and we have some big names on our cap table. So attending these association meetings resulted in not only my first round of funding but also in connecting me to Sanjeev who, till today, remains my sounding board and only mentor! I also personally mentor founders as and when I can. I have invested in fourteen start-ups and love to guide them. I just worked with one of the start-ups that is yet to turn profitable to get them debt financing this week. Sounds small but goes a long way when I talk to the bankers and help them out. I also meet other entrepreneurs who are starting out and who may need my advice and give them honest and critical feedback. This is my way of giving back to the ecosystem!

I started my company when I was twenty-one and was labelled as too young to be taken seriously. These networks helped me gain credibility. I do hope we are able to change mindsets and become a country where education and experience is respected but we stay open to the power of youth and don't judge and write them off.

The second story that shows the power of networks is one during COVID. We saw many such stories of stellar collaborations pan India, but let me tell you mine in detail. On 20 April 2021, during the second COVID wave, I was sitting absolutely numb with pain. My co-founder had just lost his father and the very same evening, my best friend also lost his father. My entire family was down with COVID and I was getting calls all day to arrange hospital beds. I was feeling utterly helpless. That's when I called The TiE Chapter of Kolkata and we formed a group, EOK (Entrepreneurs of Kolkata). We tied up with the Rotary Club to not only raise Rs 7 crore but also create a capacity of 156 beds by 12 May and 387 beds by 29 May. We used our global networks to get ventilators from Germany, and we collaborated with our army and customs networks to get materials in time. We tied up with tech entrepreneurs to get dashboards showing bed availability and worked real time with ambulance drivers to update these dashboards. A shining example of networks coming together and using their problem-solving skills to handle a crisis with no playbook. Networks work. They can create absolute magic when used effectively!

Namita: Sagar, I know this is your first time talking about your mental health issues and I am so grateful that you chose my book as the platform to do so. I want to hear not just your story but also how this made you a stronger leader and helped your company.

Sagar: Namita, I strongly believe that it is important to talk about your vulnerability and the pain in your life so that others may find strength in your example. But I will also tell you how this has actually been good for my business as well and this makes a case for many leaders to start talking about these issues more openly and with pride.

So around my eleventh grade, I realized I had obsessive compulsive disorder (OCD). Going to counsellors wasn't common in those days and I suffered in silence without much support. Over time, I realized that my quest for perfection, which is a function of OCD, was a strength in my professional life and pushed me to set high standards for myself and my team. But this very trait was a big problem in my personal life where I had a series of painful heartbreaks, always driven by my expectations of the same perfection from my partner. I was not able to accept their shortcomings. This pain at a personal level would often result in long periods of depression and also anxiety attacks. There was a time in 2019, where I had the biggest anxiety attack. I cried in the restroom and then stepped out with a smile on my face to greet the fifty-plus visitors waiting for me at my store opening.

This part of my personal life has made me a leader with a lot of empathy. I have built a culture and persona where anybody in my organization feels absolutely comfortable approaching me to discuss their concerns. I have no issues apologizing and saying 'I am sorry' when I feel I have been wrong. We have never held back or been stingy with helping our employees in need. I remember this one incident where an outsourced employee fell off a train and we spent over Rs 9 lakh to save his life. We do this for all our employees and every grateful employee gets us ten good ones when we expand. This has helped us build really strong teams and retain them! I have allowed my team to see my human, flawed side and they love me even more for it. Today, we have built a culture of empathy and compassion largely driven by my ability to show my flaws and lead from the front! Talking about this is never easy but more successful leaders need to do this and inspire others to follow suit. This is needed on a priority basis to normalize and encourage much-needed conversations around mental health!

* * *

As I ended my conversation with Sagar, I knew he had touched a deep part of my core. I had goosebumps and I was reminded of my scars and my pain and how difficult it has been to speak about them. I started this journey of speaking up about my issues just a year ago and here is a courageous entrepreneur who has started this at thirty-four. I have no doubt that this young man will go on to impact many lives with not just his entrepreneurial accolades but more importantly, with his personal stories of pain and vulnerability and will truly inspire many like him to be courageous and dream big!

Chapter 15

The Lifelong Learner

I have been very fortunate to meet very inspiring leaders in my life. They have all been competent with a string of educational qualifications, business milestones and awards to their credit. But the ones who have touched my heart and truly inspired me are the ones with humility. There was a lovely quote by Osho that keeps coming back to me. **'There are two ways and try to understand that these are the only ways. One way is to go out and prove that you are somebody, the other way is to go in and realize that you are nobody.'**

It is this humility that keeps you growing, that keeps you learning throughout your life and that is the single most important trait of leaders who see the blind spots and learn and adapt their businesses the best. If you think you know it all, you are not observant. This can lead to underestimating competitors, and macro disruptions in your industry and it can have a massive negative impact on your business.

To me, this is the most important trait that separates excellent leaders from mediocre ones. So how do we cultivate this ability to keep learning?

We don't always need to read voluminous books or spend hours with a life coach or at an overpriced seminar to feel inspired. In this rat race we have become cynical and too used to these external crutches. Sometimes, all you need is to look around and really 'observe'. If we do this, everyone around us can be a teacher, and can inspire us. If we only learn to stay open, non-judgemental and observe . . .

The ability to observe, internalize, introspect and change, that is the full circle of learning.

Let me demonstrate this through a story of who my biggest teacher at *Shark Tank India* was!

Somewhere along the way, life turns us into cynical people. A few hard knocks, disappointments, disillusionments and we start overthinking, overanalysing, over judging. I am guilty of this too. And then came along Prathamesh Sinha . . . what a grand name for this tiny ten-year-old . . . this witty, wise and wonderful ball of energy who walked through the doors of *Shark Tank India* one fine afternoon!

A breath of fresh air, a gift sent to infuse all of us with a much-forgotten innocence, positivity and sense of gratitude . . . a smile so bright that you just want to hug him and do everything he wants you to.

For the ones who haven't watched Episode 13, Prathamesh is a ten-year-old visually impaired child who joined us for one of the pitches. Right from the moment he walked in, he got straight to his job. He used the device Annie, which was his teaching aid and, with absolute expertise, demonstrated all its features and its impact on his learning. He fielded our tough questions with confidence much much beyond his years. He was unbelievably concise, clear and confident and then started the banter. He had researched on each one of us, our companies and went on to recognize all of us by our voices and then he gave us feedback on our products. Yes, you read that right! He sat on the Shark chair as if he belonged there, had been doing this for years and held our attention for a good half hour with his intelligent conversation.

Days later, I invited him to the monthly Star Brand Award event at Emcure to address my team and give away the awards. His Instagram handle reads, 'Prathamesh Sinha – Motivational Speaker'. And boy, did he motivate all of us! I interviewed him for half-an-hour and he left us laughing and teary-eyed.

I was deeply pained when I heard his story from his mother. Prathamesh wasn't born blind. He developed a tumour at fifteen months of age that left him blind for life. He has had two surgeries already for tumours that are recurring in nature (one in 2012 and one in 2019). In 2019, he had to take radiation post surgery. Since part of his pituitary gland had to be removed during the surgery, he is on lifetime medication for hormones (thyroxin and hydrocortisone). He also needs to take medicines to ensure that the tumour does not grow back. At such a young age, he is on such strong medication and yet, he keeps smiling and spreading joy wherever he goes!

As Maya Angelou says, **'You will forget what people said or did but you will never forget how they made you feel.'**

Prathamesh made us feel like a million bucks.

If you keep your eyes open, you can learn from everyone. So many inspire me every single day, to have courage and to keep going! I have so many examples from my life to demonstrate this; let me share just a couple. My house help taught me courage when she chose to be the breadwinner given an alcoholic and jobless husband. She took charge of her children's destiny and refused to give up. All the lovely ladies who came on my talk show on women's health had such painful stories but they didn't whine, cry or act like victims. Instead, they showed such strength and positivity that till today, I am inspired to stay grateful and happy.

I would like to demonstrate through an example the benefit to one's business due to such a mindset. In 2007, Emcure's business was almost 100 per cent from India but we always had aspirations of building a global company. My father is an avid reader who reads 3–4 books per month in addition to global magazines like *Time* and *The Economist*. When we started meeting partners from various countries for strategic alliances, he would instantly put them at ease by talking about their politics, current affairs, sports, and sometimes, even pop culture references. This would be a highly effective ice-breaker and a great start to a more engaging conversation.

The point I am trying to make is that the most important question we have to keep asking ourselves every single day is this: How can we keep our eyes open so that we get inspired and learn from everyone we meet? The day we learn to be humble enough to master this is the day we will have set on our journey to become lifelong learners!

Interview with Jaydeep Barman, Co-Founder and CEO, Rebel Foods

Jaydeep leads unicorn Rebel Foods. An engineer and MBA from INSEAD, he is a pioneer in the cloud kitchen space. When we started speaking, I was amazed at how he kept re-inventing himself and his company through his eleven-year journey and we both agreed that 'Lifelong Learner' is the chapter that was the best fit for his story. So let's spend time understanding how he built a unicorn with innovations and technology that are truly revolutionary in the food industry and why he calls himself a lifelong learner!

Namita: Jaydeep, let's start from the very beginning. How did you come up with the idea of starting Faasos (now Rebel Foods)?

Jaydeep: I started my journey in the start-up ecosystem with a Pune-based edtech company called Brainvisa led by Supam Maheshwari. While in Pune, I was missing my comfort food from Kolkata and started Faasos, making these wraps that I had grown up eating. It was never started as a serious business venture, just a passion project on the side. Post Brainvisa, I took a break to do my MBA at INSEAD and then worked at McKinsey in London. In 2011, I came back to India on a sabbatical and that's when I decided to truly start my entrepreneurial journey. I saw enough customer love for Faasos to want to scale it. I initially started off with a vison to scale Faasos as a restaurant business but then I realized that India has the highest rent-to-sales ratio which makes the restaurant business very challenging. Around that time, I did a simple survey where we asked our delivery customers: how many of them had seen a Faasos outlet? When 75 per cent replied that they had never been to one, it was an eye-opener for us. We realized that location doesn't matter and that's when we decided to pivot to cloud kitchen and our version of 'Internet restaurants'.

Namita: You are truly a pioneer in the cloud kitchen space and have tried many innovative strategies. What are some of these and how have they helped you scale?

Jaydeep: So, in our journey, we had three light-bulb moments. Firstly, we realized that location doesn't matter and shut down all fifty Faasos outlets. The second aha moment was when we realized that we needn't restrict ourselves to wraps and could expand to other organic brands. We launched Behrouz Biryani and Oven Story. Behrouz Biryani is the largest biryani brand in India and is the highest-rated biryani brand in Dubai. Oven Story is available in eighty cities in India and in Jakarta and Dubai as well. Faasos is available in ten countries today and is the largest wraps brand in India. Our third breakthrough moment was when we realized that just like we scaled homegrown food brands, we could do the same with third-party brands through our model. That's when we partnered with Wendy's and got an exclusive license for their brand. It took McDonalds' ten years to put up 250 stores; it took us seven months to ensure Wendy's gets to eighty locations. We will cross the 250 locations milestone in the next twelve months. Bottom line, our model helps you scale faster than any other!

Namita: This is truly fascinating! How do you think about marketing and brand building in your space?

Jaydeep: In the last few years, we have seen many strong D2C brands emerge and all these are on the strength of massive social media campaigns. It's mainly on Instagram as that's the media of choice for millennials today. We have a network of 5000 influencers. Food business is based largely on word of mouth and we have focused on the customer experience and ensuring we get the highest ratings on all platforms.

Namita: What is truly impressive is how you have used technology in your business. Can you speak more on that?

Jaydeep: Since our focus is customer experience, predictability and consistency is paramount. There are three steps in any food journey: dispensing (what to put and when), ingredients and movements (tossing, stirring, etc.). We want to standardize these three steps for consistency. We want to ensure that all locations offer the same quality and it is not dependent on the quality of chefs in those locations and their judgement call. We have a monitoring system using AI to ensure that the five metrics (size, weight, appearance, temperature and texture) are meeting the defined standards all across. To this extent, we have focused on culinary innovation and applied for six patents. Let me explain with an example. We have a patent for a smart auto fryer. The technology for fries, burger and pizza has been set globally but this is lacking for Asian food, especially Indian food. For samosas, falafel, fried chicken etc., the time of frying, amount of oil, and oil temperature are different for different food items. The auto fryer uses technology to ensure that these parameters are standardized and the food quality is the same across all locations.

Namita: How has your experience been with fundraising?

Jaydeep: We like to think of ourselves as pioneers where we are constantly innovating, trying different things, and learning on the go. There are bound to be mistakes and setbacks. We need investors who have the courage to live with this constant experimentation and failure. They need to have a long-term outlook and have to be patient investors who are in it for the long haul. We have been extremely careful while selecting our investor partners and as a result, have been fortunate to have believers and champions who support our pioneering work!

Namita: Jaydeep, you call yourself 'the lifelong learner'. Tell us why this is so important to you and how you consciously work on cultivating this trait?

Jaydeep: To me, the most important trait any leader can have is the ability to be a lifelong learner. When I think about what is the common trait in entrepreneurs who have done things differently, whether it is Jeff Bezos, Elon Musk or Steve Jobs, it is the fact that they think on 'first principle basis'. This means that they are always looking to create something new, something never done before! For them, learning and evolving is the secret sauce. I work on developing the learning muscle in four distinct ways. Firstly, I make it a point to read at least three books every single month. I have made reading an important part of our company culture. Very often, when we are stuck with a problem, we read and look at what other companies have done to learn the right lessons. For example, when we got our new head of people and culture, we read the Netflix book on 'No Rules Rules' to think through how to build and develop talent. We encourage people to read by suggesting books, and having a policy for reimbursement of books. Our offsite has mandatory pre-reading. The book picked for our upcoming offsite is on tribal leadership, which inspired Phil Jackson, the coach of Chicago Bulls, to harness the power of high ego individuals to win the NBA championship for seven seasons. Such books challenge our thinking and ensure we have great thought-provoking discussions at our offsites. Second thing I do to keep learning is that we all have several one-on-one meetings with our internal teams and customers. We ask open-ended questions and just listen and learn; learn what's going well, what's not going well, what are the challenges, and what needs to change. Third thing I do is have one-on-ones with key external leaders like investors and other founders to exchange ideas and best practices. This stimulates my thinking and I always walk away with new perspectives and ideas. Fourth, I am an avid listener and observer. For me, learning doesn't always come only from active interactions and dialogues. Just by observing how other leaders behave, and what questions they are asking can be the biggest learning tool. I have practiced all this over the years and keep working on it to get better and better at it. I want to be a lifelong learner!

Conclusion

Shark Tank India Season One started a revolution of sorts in India. Right from grandmothers to kids, all are talking about valuation and equity these days. People got a masterclass in management through storytelling. The impact of this on our country will be profound.

This book captures some of the key learnings and stories of Season One. Are they new concepts? The answer is no. But they are concepts told with new stories. These stories are from my personal and professional life; from founders I have invested in and from business leaders who have impacted my thinking and values. Hopefully, this book will inspire many to aim high.

Season Two will see more applications, stronger ventures and maybe more Sharks who will bring different perspectives. Entrepreneurs will be the new role models that everyone looks up to. This is a subject already being taught in many business schools. I dream of a day when this will be taught in schools as creative thinking, problem solving needs to start early. One thing I have learned from my entrepreneurship academy in the past six years is that our kids are ready for this. In fact, they are yearning for this level of stimulation and out-of-the-box thinking. This is a way to not just inspire them to dream big but also to break taboos around concepts like failure, gender stereotypes etc. I often get asked what I foresee as the biggest challenge our next generation will face and my answer remains mental health issues. This is a serious concern. So much can be taught in schools through entrepreneurship stories and case studies. How to stay positive and resilient in the face of failure; how a purpose-driven life can ensure stronger mental health. This is the age when children are not cynical, they are open to new concepts. Like a sponge absorbing everything good that flows towards them. I hope we see more policymaking around this, more schools take this up and we have more students who want to stay back in our country and pursue dreams of being entrepreneurs.

So go on and think through problems you see around you, and come up with ways to solve them. Entrepreneurship is the most rewarding journey and I hope all of you are ready for this helluva roller-coaster ride!

Acknowledgements

I would like to thank all my family members and my mentors who supported me through this incredible journey. I would like to thank Sanjeev Bikhchandani of Info Edge and Sandeep Murthy of Lightbox Ventures who guided me on developing my investment framework.

Thank you, Supam Maheshwari, Sahil Barua, Sagar Daryani, Jaydeep Barman, Bimal Unnikrishnan and Sanjeev Bikhchandani once again for letting me feature your journeys.

A big hug to the lovely founders from *Shark Tank India*—Rano, Aditi, Aishwarya, Sanskriti, Devang and Shachi—I am so proud to pen down our conversations here. I have also quoted examples from Marico and Bajaj Auto. Thank you, Mr Harsh Mariwala and Mr Rajiv Bajaj, for giving me the creative liberty to do so.

Most importantly, heartfelt gratitude to my friends and well-wishers who read through the draft and suggested edits. Sahil Barua, Hitendra Singh, Promila Ayyangar, Mrinali Mirchandani and Mr Vijay Gokhake, thank you for taking the time to suggest ways in which I could make the book more relevant and stronger.

Thank you to the Sony and Studio Next teams for this opportunity and my co-sharks without whom this experience would not have been so enjoyable and memorable. I reserve my biggest thank you for all the founders I met on the show, who taught me so much and inspired me beyond what words can describe!

Appendix I

Summary of All Pitches on *Shark Tank India* Season One

S.No	Company	Product/Solution	Funded
1	BluePine Industries	Convenient, innovative, Himalayan food start-up (handcrafted Momos)	YES
2	Booz Scooters	Electric mobility for commercial premises and leisure sports	YES
3	Heart Up My Sleeve	A homegrown luxury fashion label that curates transformable clothing with minimalism and sustainability at the core	YES
4	Tagz Foods	Uber premium urban GenZ snacking experiences	YES
5	Head and Heart	Developmental counsellor with an electric approach to therapy and a passion for nature, travel, psychology & science	NO
6	Agro Tourism	Agricultural service and tourism founded by 'father of agri-tourism in India', Mr Pandurang Taware	NO
7	Qzense Labs	Transforming the fresh food supply chain with data	NO
8	Peeschute	A revolutionary unisex pocket-sized toilet	YES
9	NOCD	It's not a drink; it's a lifestyle. A recreational drink to accelerate metabolism and cognitive function	YES

10	CosIQ	High performance skincare using effective clinical technologies with a focus on clean ingredients, functional actives, minimalist formulations and real, visible results	YES
11	JhaJi Achaar	Authentic, homemade pickles made by women from Mithilanchal in Bihar	NO
12	Bummer	Ultra-soft comfort wear that shout fun, fit ridiculously well and feel like heaven	YES
13	Revamp Moto	Electric bikes built on modular utility platforms	YES
14	Hungry Heads	A concept restaurant, serves Maggie and more in 80+ flavours	NO
15	Shrawani Engineers	Shrawani Engineers is a Nagpur-based company manufacturing and procuring different types of body shaping products like belly button shaper kit	NO
16	Skippi Pops	India's first ice pop brand is made with 100 per cent RO water, natural colours and flavours	YES
17	Menstrupedia	World's most innovative way to teach/learn about menstruation & India's first comic book on periods	YES

18	Hecolll	Manufacturer of proprietary cotton fabric which blocks 99% UV rays, filters 95 per cent pollution, inhibits viruses and bacteria upon contact	NO
19	Raising Superstars	Child development app: Unlock your 0–3-year-old baby's potential with five-minute activities	YES
20	Torch-it	Empowering the differently-abled community with innovative and affordable assistive aids	NO
21	La Kheer Deli	Serving gourmet 'kheer' like never before	NO
22	Beyond Snack	The tastiest banana chips in the world	YES
23	Vivalyf Innovations – Easy Life	A non-invasive glucose monitoring system (EZLYF) and app that bring affordability, accuracy and a variety of features to help people with diabetes	YES
24	Motion Breeze	World's first adaptive, intelligent electric motorcycle	YES
25	Altor	India's own smart motorcycle helmets	YES
26	Ariro	Wooden toys and aids for 0–3-year-olds	YES
27	Kabira Handmad	Range of cold pressed cooking/industrial oils and allied products	NO

28	Nuutjob	A range of men's intimate hygiene products for all 'downstairs needs'	YES
29	Meatyour	D2C brand delivering fresh free range odorless eggs to your doorstep	YES
30	EventBeep	Student community app – Making student life beautiful	YES
31	Gopal's 56	Fiber-based, healthier ice cream	NO
32	ARRCOAT Surface Textures	Made in India, 0 VOC surface décor – extending your personality on to your walls	YES
33	Farda	Premium, customized streetwear brand for people who are not afraid to make a statement	YES
34	Auli Lifestyle	Indulgent, luxurious, organic – AULI isn't just about the products that pamper and prime you to look and feel your best, AULI is a lifestyle and wellness statement	YES
35	SweeDesi	Bringing authentic, traditional flavours from their origin to your doorstep in twenty-four hours, absolutely fresh	NO
36	LOKA	India's first multiplayer gamified virtual metaverse based on 3D maps of real-world cities and locations	YES
37	Annie	World's first self-learning Braille literacy device	YES

38	Caragreen	Providing healthy materials to help you build better	YES
39	The Yarn Bazaar	A holistic B2B yarn platform offering trading, lending and logistics services, all under one roof	YES
40	The Renal Project	A chain of micro-dialysis service centres	YES
41	Morikko Pure Foods	Nutritious dried fruit snacks for your health and wellness	NO
42	Good Good Piggy Bank	Ed-fintech startup that helps and teaches new generations to manage money digitally	NO
43	Hammer Lifestyle	D2C and an FMEG (Fast moving electronic goods) brand dealing in fast-paced lifestyle gadgets	YES
44	PNT	Smart, customized robotics solutions provider undertaking industrial projects based on AI, ML, ROS and IoT robotics	YES
45	Cocofit	Coconut-based beverage and ice cream franchise	YES
46	Bamboo India	Daily use bamboo products as a perfect replacement to plastic products	YES
47	Flying Furr	Paid grooming and spa-on-wheels at your home, for pet dogs	NO

48	Beyond Water	Liquid water enhancer aimed at health, convenience as a go-to drink using natural highest-quality ingredients	YES
49	Let's Try	Healthy and fun snacking with no preservatives, no artificial flavours, colours, transfat or cholesterol	YES
50	Find Your Kicks India	One-stop destination for buying and selling hyped sneakers and apparels	YES
51	Aas Vidyalaya	India's first online school for grades 6–10 across education boards like CBSE, NIOS, UP, Maharashtra, Bihar, MP and Rajasthan	YES
52	Outbox	Private candlelight dinners, extravagant proposals and personalized gifts	NO
53	RoadBounce	Pothole detection software and data that helps you detect road conditions using any smartphone	YES
54	Mommy's Kitchen	Italian dishes; specializing in thin crust pizzas	NO
55	India Hemp and Co	Medical cannabis wellness and hemp nutrition products	NO
56	Otua	Electric auto vehicle	YES

57	Anthyesti	Professional funeral services present across fifty cities in India	NO
58	Ethik	India's first premium non-leather fashion brand for men	NO
59	WeSTOCK	Agritech start-up with products for livestock health monitoring and tracking using high-end technology	YES
60	KetoIndia	Customized Indian keto diets for various medical issues	NO
61	Magic Lock	LPG commercial and domestic gas safety devices	NO
62	The State Plate	Sourcing 100 per cent authentic regional food products and delivering across India	YES
63	Bakarmax	Digital creators; comics and animation studio	NO
64	IN A CAN	Premium cocktails, universally loved flavours – in a can	YES
65	Get a Whey	Sugar-free ice cream packed with proteins	YES
66	Sid 07 Designs	Astute engineering and designs to create product solutions	YES
67	The Quirky Nari	A quirky, fun and edgy line of customized apparels for women	YES
68	Hair Originals	Exporters of natural hair extensions and wigs globally	YES
69	Poo de Cologne	Pre-toilet spray with essential oils which is pure, natural and safe	NO

70	Moonshine Meadery	Asia's and India's first meadery (mead is a gluten-free alcoholic beverage)	NO
71	Falhari	One-stop shop for healthy snacking and fresh eating	NO
72	Namhya Foods	An effort to bring back the golden heritage of long-forgotten basic Indian food that blends with today's lifestyle	YES
73	Urban Monkey	New-age Indian streetwear unisex clothing brand for men and women in India	NO
74	Guardian Gears	Manufacturer of premium luggage for motorcycles and touring including backpacks, tank bags, saddle bags, tail bags and accessories	NO
75	Modern Myth	E-commerce label of handcrafted vegan bags from India	NO
76	The Sass Bar	India's first soapery making soaps that looks like desserts	YES
77	KG Agrotech	A start-up that makes products related to agriculture; their flagship product helps in pesticide spraying, seeding and carrying material	YES
78	Nuskha Kitchen	Maternity medicinal edibles	NO

79	PawsIndia	Pawsindia is the most preferred online shopping place for pet owners and pet lovers looking for new and top line products and supplies	YES
80	Sunfox Technologies	Working actively in the area of developing biomedical devices (portable ECG) for cardiovascular diseases, hypertension, asthma	YES
81	Alpino	Wide variety of convenient, delicious and affordable food choices that can help everyone enjoy a balanced and healthy diet	NO
82	Isak Fragrances	Contemporary fragrance brand, offering best and progressive perfumery trends for men and women in India	YES
83	Julaa Automation	Automated cradle with Bluetooth connectivity, weighing scale, app-activated lullabies and tyre system	NO
84	Rare Planet	Provides a huge platform for incredible talent to showcase their handicraft creativity	YES
85	Theka Coffee	Freshly brewed Arabic coffee served in beer bottles	NO
86	Watt Technovations	Ventilation system for PPE suit wearers, smartly designed to provide user-friendly experiences	YES

87	Aliste Technologies	Provides your home with affordable, end-to-end home automation solutions	NO
88	Insurance Samadhan	Platform to resolve insurance complaints in India	YES
89	Humpy A2	Organic, A2 certified, supports climate smart farming, Indian cow-centric farming and provides 100 per cent pure organic products	YES
90	Kunafa World	A traditional Middle Eastern dessert	NO
91	Gold Safe Solutions Ind.	Suicide prevention devices ; anti-suicide fan rod	YES
92	Wakao Foods	India's first brand that makes products from jackfruit	YES
93	PDD Falcon	Internationally certified food grade stainless steel range of lunchboxes, drinkware, kitchen storage & tools	NO
94	PlayBox TV	Get access to wise range of entertainment, anytime, anywhere	NO
95	Sippline Drinking Shields	Oral hygiene product used on the rims of glasses, cups, mugs to avoid lips touching the rim of the glass while drinking	NO

96	Kabaddi Adda	Adda for all Kabaddi enthusiasts looking for Kabaddi news, videos, players interviews, match reports, insights	YES
97	Shades of Spring	500+ varieties of farm fresh flowers from Indian farmers	NO
98	Scholify	Edtech company which provides scholarships to students for studies	NO
99	Scrapshala	Interlink art, creativity and waste into sustainable functional products handcrafted by local Indian artisans	NO
100	Sabjikothi	Wheel mountable storage for transportation of fresh fruits and vegetables	NO
101	AyuRythm	Holistic wellness mobile app that works on principles of ancient Indian Ayurveda	YES
102	Astrix	WiFi and Bluetooth-enabled smart door locks	NO
103	Thea and Sid	Proposal Solutions – jewellery for every memorable moment	NO
104	Experential Etc	Experiential marketing agency in India that develops world-class experiences	NO
105	GrowFitter	Incentivized wellness platform	YES

106	Med Tech	Committed to bringing innovation in ophthalmic product ranges to help customers monitor their health conveniently	NO
107	Colour Me Mad	Provider of ten-minute customized insoles for every footwear	YES
108	Mavi's	Vegan, fermented foods and drinks	NO
109	Tweek Labs	Sports technology company that aims to bring high performance sports infrastructure and knowledge to sports organizations	YES
110	Proxgy	Provides real-time multiway collaboration between people across the globe with a distinct advantage over existing solutions	YES
111	Nomad Food Project	Ready-to-eat bacon thecha (jams)	YES
112	Twee in One	Eco-friendly brand offering two looks in one clothing	NO
113	Green Protein	Movement to promote ecological alternatives for satisfying our daily protein needs (plant-based protein)	NO
114	On2Cook	Revolutionary patent-granted (US) smart cooking device	NO
115	Jain Shikanji	Shikanji made with freshest lemons, and good quality masala which gives it its iconic delicious taste	YES

116	Woloo	Loo-discovery app that helps women locate nearest clean, safe and hygienic washroom	NO
117	Elcare India	A socially conscious healthcare services start-up, with an aim to provide high-quality elderly care, security, and convenience services	NO
118	Sneakare	Integrates sneaker culture with latest technology to offer a wide range of accessories and sneaker care products	YES
119	Storemygoods	Hassle-free, customized, and affordable storage solutions for individuals, start-ups and businesses	YES
120	French Crown	India's first sustainable fast fashion brand in premium menswear category	NO
121	Devnagri	India's first AI-powered human translation platform for Indian languages	NO

Appendix II

How to Get Selected for *Shark Tank India*: An Interview with Bimal Unnikrishnan, Show Runner (*Shark Tank India*)

Namita: My compliments for a spectacular show that has taken the nation by storm. Would love to hear about the journey from you. Let's start with the selection process for Season One. You got us the most incredible stories, how did you select these?

Bimal: We invited applications in June 2021. We got over 68,000 applications. They had filled the application form with details of their venture (mainly personal journey, sector, business details and stage of business: pre-revenue or revenue stage) and this wasn't easy. Time was a constraint not only for us but for every department including the tech, marketing and sales teams. There were challenges around trust deficit (founders were worried about the privacy of their business data), legal compliances and follow-up calls for missing data. We managed to work around all this and got a good diversity of ventures across industries, regions and gender representations. There was a sixteen-member cross-functional team with experts from our creative, production and business divisions. We narrowed this to 5000 applicants and finally 1000 who were auditioned across three cities—Bengaluru, Delhi and Mumbai. Our teams spent endless hours filtering and reviewing audition videos to narrow it down to 300 that were finally selected for the show. This entire process went on till 8 September. Since this is a global show, we had a global SOP in place, but needless to say, we had to tweak it to suit the Indian sensibilities.

Namita: The founders seemed so confident, well prepared, super dramatic and interesting when they pitched to us. How did you prep them for this?

Bimal: I strongly believe that 'talent selects itself'. Our 300 shortlisted ventures were fantastic. They were driven and creative, and many came up with the drama quotient themselves. For example, the act by Beyond Snacks banana chips—the way he tore his t-shirt, got the Kathakali dancer, etc. was all his own creativity. For others, our creative team had to spend hours prepping them, right from what they should wear, and how to create a 'splash' that holds the attention of the Sharks. Taking care of their travel, and scheduling all this took hours of planning and individual detailing. Sharks would typically wind up their shoot by

9 pm but our team stayed on for hours post that, preparing for the next day. I don't think any of us slept much!

Namita: The scheduling was flawless. As Sharks, we had a super-efficient experience. How did you go about that?

Bimal: For every three-day schedule, we had to really think through the 'batching'—what pitches would be shown on each day such that there was enough diversity, interest and the right number of deals per day to keep the Sharks engaged! We would schedule food pitches right before lunch, for example. Also, we had to be efficient with the time between pitches such that the Sharks didn't have to wait for too long. Anybody who saw the gorgeous product displays wouldn't believe the record time in which we set them up between pitches!

Namita: There has been certain flak or criticism of the process. What are some that you have heard and what are your thoughts around them?

Bimal: There were social media discussions on how some of the participants weren't sure till the last minute on whether they were accepted or not. This was a small number but created enough negative buzz. We will just have to tighten the planning and communication process the next time round. Not all 198 pitches made it to television, but that's media. We had to showcase the most interesting ones and the ones that people could relate to and learn from. The dropouts knew ahead of time that there were many that would not make it. There was full disclosure. There were constant allegations that the show was scripted, and it's absolutely untrue, but after a while, you stop listening and responding to all this and stay focused on the job at hand.

Namita: There were also questions around why some pitches such as Gopal 56 with a valuation of Rs 1200 crore or the belly button shaper made it to the show? What was the objective behind showcasing some of these pitches?

Bimal: One must realize that this show was the first of its kind in India, a category creation of sorts and a lot of education was needed for the masses. This could only be done through story telling. Showing crazy valuations and why the Sharks found the valuation ridiculous was a learning in itself and an important one that needed to be shown. For the belly button shaper, it was a combination of entertainment plus the fact that such ideas can sell 600 units too! We need to see all kinds of ideas and have the audience learn the right lessons in entrepreneurship.

Namita: How did you adapt this show to Indian sensibilities while still working within the global framework and global legal compliances?

Bimal: All of us on the team have been part of very successful TV shows. So that experience had taught us that 'humanizing' the show and preserving the authenticity of people on it, go a long way in being able to connect with the audience. So, we focused on getting the pitches and the personal journeys (of both the pitchers and the Sharks) right. Indians love a bit of glitter so the set was much larger and more glamourous than the US version of the show, and it was the same with how our Sharks looked.

Namita: How was the response from the various stakeholders, especially the sponsors? It was a risk in a sense, not being a typical dance, drama or comedy show that masses are used to?

Bimal: Fortunately for us, most business leaders were aware of this concept and were very enthused about bringing this to India and being a part of it! We had no issues with buy-in and collaborations.

Namita: What are some of the things you would change in Season Two?

Bimal: I will ensure that my team has a better work-life balance. The team really had to put in long hours and I applaud their commitment to the cause and resilience through all those months! I would like to do a better job of resource allocation and work distribution so that the team has a better experience next time. Not just my team but this is true for everyone—programming, tech, marketing, operations and sales teams. The tech turnaround time was really short, so that was a big challenge. Leveraging technology to make the application process and data collection more efficient is another area that needs work! We need to start planning for Season Two much more in advance.

Namita: So the million-dollar question: Will there be a Season Two? When?

Bimal: Well, wait and watch . . .

Appendix III

भारत की बेटियाँ

A heartfelt poem that I have penned for all the lovely ladies who dare to dream big!

खुद पे तुझे क्यों है कम विश्वास?
तू और सिर्फ तू बदल सकती है ये एहसास

बहुत दूर है तुझे जाना
बहुत कुछ है हासिल करना

चाहे कोई दे या ना दे तेरा साथ
तुझे खुद करनी होगी एक नयी शुरुआत

अपने दिल की सुन, दुनिया की ना कर परवाह
अपनी मेहनत से बना अपनी एक खास जगह

साहस और सच्चाई से जी, खुद को बना इतना काबिल
हर एक मंज़िल कर पाओगी तुम हासिल

दूर करो मन से ये शिकवे गिले
अपनी तक़दीर खुद बनाओ, किसी का साथ मिले ना मिले

जीने में लाओ अनुशासन
शांत रखना सीखो अपना मन

मत कोसो अपने हाथों की लकीर,
खुद लिखो तुम अपनी तक़दीर

कथनी और करनी रखो एक सी
याद रखो, तुम हो अनोखी, ना कोई और है तुम जैसी

चेहरे पर रखो हमेशा हँसी, दिल में सुकून
हर एक मंज़िल की ओर बढ़ो लेकर हिम्मत, हौंसला
और जूनून

दुनिया चाहे लगाये कितनी भी बेड़ियाँ
चाहे ढूंढे तुझमे कितनी भी कमियाँ

बनो खुद की ताकत, करती रहो कोशिश
कभी हार ना मानना, यही है एक गुज़ारिश।

Appendix IV

My Favourite Books

1. *Life in Full*: Indra Nooyi
2. *Becoming*: Michelle Obama
3. *The Moment of Lift*: Melinda Gates
4. *Hard Things About Hard Things*: Ben Horowitz
5. *Shoe Dog*: Phil Knight
6. *Dream With Your Eyes Open*: Ronnie Screwvala
7. *Harsh Realities*: Harsh Mariwala
8. *What it Takes*: Stephen A. Schwarzman
9. *Creativity Inc.*: Ed Catmull
10. *Marketing Warfare*: Al Ries
11. *Lean In*: Sheryl Sandberg
12. *Originals*: Adam Grant
13. *Light on Life*: K.S. Iyengar
14. *A Shot at History*: Abhinav Bindra
15. *Only the Paranoid Survive*: Andy Grove

Appendix V

My Favourite Quotes

Manzil milegi bhatak kar hi sahi,
Gumrah to wo hain jo ghar se nikle hi nahi.
Ghalib

I've learned that people will forget what you said, people will forget what you did, but people will never forget how you made them feel.
Maya Angelou

After all, the Universe is made up of stories and not atoms.
Muriel Rukeyser

Keep looking and don't settle. As with all matters of the heart you will know when you find it.
Steve Jobs

The highest reward for man's toil is not what he gets for it, but what he becomes by it.
John Ruskin

You never get a second chance to make a first impression.
Unknown

The smallest act of kindness is worth more than the greatest intention.
Khalil Gibran

Whatever you resist, persists.
Carl Jung

Whenever you have a setback, ask yourself the right question. Not why is this happening to me, but what is this here to teach me.
Oprah Winfrey

Feelings are really your GPS system for Life.
Oprah Winfrey

To lead an orchestra, you must turn your back on the crowd.
Unknown

Don't let the noise of others' opinion drown out your own inner voice.
Steve Jobs

Be the change you want to see.
Mahatma Gandhi

The true leader is always led.
Carl Jung

Courage is the first of human qualities because it is the
quality which guarantees the others.
Aristotle

To belittle, you have to be little.
Khalil Gibran

The teacher who is indeed wise does not bid you to
enter the house of his wisdom but rather leads you to the
threshold of your mind.
Khalil Gibran

Umr bhar Ghalib ye hi bhool karta raha,
Dhool chehre pe thi aur aina saaf karta raha.
Ghalib

Life is not measured by the number of breaths we take but
by the moments that take our breath away.
Maya Angelou

To lead people, walk behind them.
Lao Tzu

A leader is best when people barely know he exists, when
his work is done, his aim fulfilled, they say we did it
ourselves.
Lao Tzu

My mission in life is not merely to survive, but to thrive;
and to do so with some passion, some compassion, some
humor and some style.
Maya Angelou

There are two ways, and try to understand that these are
the only ways. One way is to go out and prove that you

are somebody; the other way is to go in and realize that you are nobody.
OSHO

What do you never leave your home without—an idea.
Rajiv Bajaj, Managing Director, Bajaj Auto

Failures are a part and parcel of an entrepreneur's journey. Sometimes, you win and sometimes, you learn.
Harsh Mariwala, Chairman, Marico

Everybody can be great ... because anybody can serve. You don't have to have a college degree to serve. You don't have to make your subject and verb agree to serve. You only need a heart full of grace. A soul generated by love.
Martin Luther King

Appendix VI

Biggest Myths About an Entrepreneur

1. **Entrepreneurs don't have a personal life**: It's true that unlike a corporate job, entrepreneurship is a 24/7 job. However, it's incorrect to visualize an entrepreneur as a harrowed, unhappy person buried in work with no personal life. Entrepreneurs need to stay sharp and for that, they need to reduce the risk of burnout by scheduling balance in their lives. One of the key benefits of being an entrepreneur is that you control your schedule and have more flexibility than others. Making a to-do list on your phone every morning, prioritizing and delegating helps.

2. **Founder myths**: One often hears of biases like husband-wife founder teams are risky, having too many co-founders is risky, etc. One cannot make such generalizations. Truth be told, it all depends on the quality of the team, their relationship, clarity of roles and their commitment levels. There are

other founder myths such as founders have to be young and from big cities, founders are born and not made, etc. Again, there are enough examples to debunk these myths.

3. **Entrepreneurs don't have a boss**: Most entrepreneurs end up diluting their stake in multiple rounds of fundraising and end up having a minority stake. Investors end up having a majority stake and founders are very much answerable to these investors as well as the board at large. After all, we have often heard cases of investors replacing founders as CEOs with professionals who might be better qualified to run the larger business.

4. **Entrepreneurs don't exit**: In fact, it's the opposite. Good founders know when to pivot an existing business or shut down and start anew. Knowing when to walk away is a very important skill and takes a lot of mental discipline.

5. **Founders must have strong engineering and/or management degrees**: This isn't always true. We have enough examples of people without expert degrees who have built large, successful businesses. Also, you may have a degree in a particular function but find your calling in a different area. Aman Gupta, my co-Shark, recently posted the following on his LinkedIn profile which best explains this point: 'Boat's Chief Marketing Officer hasn't studied marketing. The Chief Product Officer isn't an engineer and their Chief Financial Officer isn't a Chartered Accountant. We believe in letting people follow their passion. We believe in doing what floats your boat.'

Appendix VII

My Struggles as a Parent

Children are a gift, many of us are fortunate to get handed healthy and happy babies. How do we mess up and turn them into anxious adults? Twenty per cent adolescents have some form of mental illness and 70 per cent don't get diagnosed and treated on time. I am certain that this statistic is much higher post the COVID pandemic.

I have personally gone through a rough time with my two boys (Vir, sixteen; Jai, eleven) and wanted to share some of my insights, some learnings which I wish I had internalized and adopted much earlier. I hope this helps at least a few struggling parents like me and especially working mothers.

So here are my top six learnings.

1) **Stand up for yourself and speak up**: I had the luxury of coming back from my office by 4.30 p.m. and logging in at night to catch up on work. I could

control my own travel schedule which I restricted to 3–4 days a month. I tried my best to not miss any school events, worked hard at staying active with school mothers, diligently arranged play dates, birthday parties and took an hour of their studies every single day for the past ten years regardless of my own anxiety or fatigue levels. Yet in spite of my best efforts, several well-meaning family members and friends for the last sixteen years have consistently labelled me 'absentee mom' 'self-absorbed mom'. Things changed when my kids who were used to hearing these labels started calling me that. This is when I had had enough and decided to speak up and ask people to stop labelling me. My advice: if you feel you have done the best you can, speak up and don't allow people to put you down. In my case, as a mother I would rate myself a 7/10 in competence and a 10/10 in love demonstrated, that's okay, that's good enough. But still I stayed quiet when these labels were put to avoid unpleasantness. I wish I had stood up for myself much sooner and asked them to stop putting these labels on me.

2) **Let your children guide you**: I am a type-A personality, I like to be in the driver's seat and with all the good intent in my heart, I decided what's best for my children. This controlling (you calling the shots) behaviour is acceptable till they are ten, post that it should be about treating them as adults and making decisions based on their cues, their needs, their body language. For example, I should have shifted my older son who is prone to getting exam anxiety to an IB curriculum much sooner

than having to deal with a traumatic ICSE board experience. He gave me all the signs but I had my blinders on and did what I wanted, not what he was so clearly telling me he wanted. So, start listening more.

3) **Work–life balance and involvement of both parents:** Stop saying 'I work long hours, I travel a lot, I don't have time for my family' as a badge of honour, especially fathers. So many fathers have proudly announced to me at parties that they don't even know what grade their child is in, they haven't changed a single diaper ever. It's infuriating to see such ignorance. Children need involvement of both parents for their mental health. It's about time school WhatsApp groups included fathers too and companies adopted work–life balance policies as a conscious investment in generation next.

4) **Stop judging them by external parameters:** I have been guilty of this. Under the garb of instilling drive, I have told my son he must aspire for Harvard, shown him pictures of the university, compared him to other kids, offered rewards for a certain percentage in exams. This is a sure shot way to bring up insecure kids with low self-esteem. If you see signs of confidence being impacted, go to a counsellor immediately. These are trained medical experts who can be good facilitators. Often, we don't seek timely help as we still bother about the world and perceive such help as a taboo, a flaw. I have taken counselling myself and have taken various family members for counselling when needed and strongly advocate this. In summary, the best parenting lesson here

is from my friend Raju Hirani's movie *3 Idiots*.
How beautifully he showed that what's most important is to let the child do what they want, what
makes them happy and not what society feels is
right for them.

5) **The hard truth about discipline:** I have raised my
voice, justified physical aggression, verbal abuse
saying its occasional and needed and oh well, our
parents did it and look, we turned out great! This
is the biggest damage you can do. **As Rumi says,
raise your words, not your voice. It is rain that
grows flowers, not thunder!** Love and connec-
tion are the only way to help your child learn and
grow. Our insecurities, our short temper, our need
for instant results, our ego, our high expectations,
basically our shortcomings make us mete out harsh
punishments when every statistic, case study and
our own experience and instinct has demonstrated that respecting them, treating them as adults,
lovingly showing the consequences of their wrong
actions and letting them fail and learn are the best
ways to discipline and teach. Let them fail and then
teach them to focus on the learning and not guilt.

6) **Live in the moment:** I am always on my phone,
under the garb of work messages, I do spend a de-
cent time on social media, chatting with friends
which is perfectly fine but this makes most kids
these days feel unheard. Keep designated time for
phone, work emails and tell your children about
these time slots. Rest of the time, live in the present and enjoy them. Not in the past trying to remind them of their mistakes or the future, trying to

explain your expectations for the hundredth time, but just focus on the moment so you can be non-judgemental, non-preachy and not just enjoy them but more importantly you pick up the right cues from them and teach them what is needed most in that moment.

Recently I lost control with my teen in a public place, I yelled at him and humiliated him in public as I felt insulted by him and my ego took over. I still can't forget the hurt in his eyes after I did this. I have never felt more awful, I felt like a big failure in life. It is important in such moments to instantly apologize once you calm down but it is most important to forgive yourself and not beat yourself up. You need to show empathy and love for yourself too. Learning and continuing to try is so much better than constantly beating yourself up and living with constant guilt. I messed up big time but that incident inspired me to write this article about my struggles which hopefully will make other parents feel a bit better and forgiving of their pain and struggles which is an intrinsic part and parcel of parenthood!

Fortunately, my husband has been more sorted as a parent and has helped bridge some of my gaps. Bottom line, if you are happy and at peace, you can be a much better parent. Most importantly, you can demonstrate to your child the most important lesson—you will continue making mistakes, having setbacks, failing, but it is important to look at this positively, as a learning experience, focus on the growth and not the hurt and most importantly, continue staying happy and grateful, no matter what!

Glossary

Glossary			
#	Chapter	Word	Meaning
1	Why This Book	Franchise	A franchise (or franchising) is a method of distributing products or services involving a franchisor, who establishes the brand's trademark or trade name and a business system, and a franchisee, who pays a royalty and often an initial fee for the right to do business under the franchisor's name and system. Domino's and Pizza Hut are prime examples of this model.
2	My Investment Framework	Proof of concept	A proof of concept is meant to determine the feasibility of the idea or to verify that the idea will function as envisioned.
3	My Investment Framework	Circle of competence	A circle of competence is the subject area which matches a person's skills or expertise. Source: https://www.berkshirehathaway.com/letters/1996.html

4	Perfect Your Pitch	TAM	Total addressable market, also called total available market, is a term that is typically used to reference the market size available for a product or service.
5	Perfect Your Pitch	Gross margin	Gross margin is the difference between revenue and cost of goods sold, divided by revenue.
6	Perfect Your Pitch	Shelf life	Shelf life is the length of time that a product may be stored without becoming unfit for use.
7	Perfect Your Pitch	SKU	A stock keeping unit is the unique type of item for sale. A product can have multiple SKUs. Eg., a dress has multiple size options, so each option is an SKU that can be sold independently.
8	Perfect Your Pitch	Sales mix	The sales mix is a calculation that determines the proportion of each type of product a business sells relative to total sales.
9	Perfect Your Pitch	Prototype stage	The prototype stage is when you create a sample product or service to test the market for customer feedback pre-launch.

10	Perfect Your Pitch	Valuation	Valuation is a quantitative process of determining the buying price of an asset or a firm.
11	You've Got the Deal, What Next?	Drag rights	Drag-along right is a legal concept in corporate law. If a shareholder with drag rights wants to sell their stake, they have the right to force the remaining minority shareholders to sell their shares.
12	You've Got the Deal, What Next?	Tag rights	When a founder is selling their share, the shareholder with tag rights has the right to sell their shares too.
13	You've Got the Deal, What Next?	Founder lock-in	A founder is 'locked in' when they are not permitted to trade a security for a mutually agreed period.
14	You've Got the Deal, What Next?	Reserve matters	Reserved matters are matters that require prior consent of investors before a decision is taken over them. For example, hiring CXOs.

| 15 | You've Got the Deal, What Next? | Exit rights | This clause defines the rights of the investors when it comes to exiting, including time period and mechanisms of exit. Some mechanisms to provide exit to investors include: through IPO (company gets listed and investor shares are sold) or Buyback (Company buys back the shares held by the investor or Strategic Sale (Company is sold to a bigger player in the same industry). |
| 16 | You've Got the Deal, What Next? | CCPS | These are Compulsorily Convertible Preference Shares that compulsorily convert into Equity Shares of the issuing company after a predetermined period. The terms of conversion are also pre-decided at the time of issue. They are recorded in the cap-table of the company and have higher and preferential rights over ordinary equity shareholders. |

| 17 | You've Got the Deal, What Next? | iSAFE | It is an Indian version of SAFE (Simple Agreement for Future Equity) that are popular investment tools in US. They are typically used at the very early rounds where it is difficult to value the company so the investor instead gives an amount of money and defines that they would get x% of future equity when company reaches a stage when it can be valued properly. |
| 18 | You've Got the Deal, What Next? | Representations and Warranties | Warranties are declarations from sellers/founders to make disclosures that declare the current understanding of various issues related to the business. For example the founder ensures that the financial statement of the company shows the true and fair view of the organization's business standings. |

19	You've Got the Deal, What Next?	Indemnification	Indemnity rights are used to protect the investing shareholder against specific losses and business claims that may arise after the deal. For example, companies buy insurance to offset losses against any unforeseen event.
20	Building Big Brands	Novelty factor	The quality of being new, fresh and interesting.
21	Building Big Brands	Market research	Market research is an organized effort to gather information about target markets and customers.
22	Building Big Brands	Pivoting	When a business pivots, it means that it's changing some aspect of its core product/s or service/s. For example, Zomato starting dine-in services after predominantly delivering food.
23	Building Big Brands	USP	A unique selling proposition or unique selling point is a factor that differentiates a product from its competitors, such as the lowest cost, the highest quality or the first-ever product of its kind.

24	Building Big Brands	Moat	This term refers to a business' ability to maintain a competitive advantage over its competitors in order to protect its long-term profits and market share.
25	Building Big Brands	CAC	Customer acquisition cost (CAC) is the amount of money a company spends to get a new customer. It helps measure the return on investment of efforts to grow their clientele.
26	Building Big Brands	AOV	Average Order Value (AOV) is an e-commerce metric that measures the average total of every order placed with a merchant over a defined period of time.
27	Building Big Brands	LTV of customer	Customer lifetime value is the total worth of a customer to a business over the whole period of their relationship. It's an important metric as it costs less to keep existing customers than it does to acquire new ones. So increasing the value of your existing customers is a great way to drive growth.

28	Building Big Brands	Repeat customer	Repeat customers are people who buy from you time and again and would be considered loyal to your brand.
29	Women Leaders Breaking Barriers	Contingency plan	A contingency plan is a plan devised for an outcome other than in the usual plan.
30	Challenges for Women Leaders	Crowdfunding	Crowdfunding is the practice of funding a project or venture by raising money from a large number of people. In modern times, it is typically done via the Internet.
31	The Vulnerable Leader	Bootstrapped	Bootstrapping describes a situation in which a founder starts a company with little capital, relying on their own money and profits from business being put back into it.
32	Leadership Mantras	Internal Rate of Return (IRR)	It is a method of estimating the profitability of an investment. It is called internal because it excludes external factors such as risk-free rate, inflation, cost of capital, or financial risk.